C000102055

BANK MERGERS

Bank Mergers

Lessons for the Future

Steven I. Davis

First published in Great Britain 2000 by
MACMILLAN PRESS LTD
Houndmills, Basingstoke, Hampshire RG21 6XS and London
Companies and representatives throughout the world

A catalogue record for this book is available from the British
Library.
ISBN 0–333–91260–8

 First published in the United States of America 2000 by
ST. MARTIN'S PRESS, LLC,
Scholarly and Reference Division,
175 Fifth Avenue, New York, N.Y. 10010

ISBN 0–312–23552–6

Library of Congress Cataloging-in-Publication Data

Davis, Steven I.
    Bank mergers: lessons for the future / Steven I. Davis
    p. cm.
    Includes bibliographical references and index.
    ISBN 0–312–23552–6 (cloth)
    1. Bank mergers—Case studies. I. Title.

HG1722 .D38 2000
332.1′6—dc21

00–042061

© Steven I. Davis 2000

All rights reserved. No reproduction, copy or transmission of this publication may be
made without written permission.

No paragraph of this publication may be reproduced, copied or transmitted save with
written permission or in accordance with the provisions of the Copyright, Designs and
Patents Act 1988, or under the terms of any licence permitting limited copying issued by
the Copyright Licensing Agency, 90 Tottenham Court Road, London WIP 0LP.

Any person who does any unauthorized act in relation to this publication may be liable to
criminal prosecution and civil claims for damages.

The author has asserted his right to be identified as the author of this work in accordance
with the Copyright, Designs and Patents Act 1988.

This book is printed on paper suitable for recycling and made from fully managed and
sustained forest sources.

10 9   8   7   6   5   4   3   2
09 08 07 06 05 04 03 02 01

Printed and bound in Great Britain
by Antony Rowe Ltd, Chippenham, Wiltshire

To my colleagues at DIBC – for their support, understanding and wonderful contribution over the past two decades.

Contents

List of Figures and Tables

Figures

Tables

Preface

The topic of bank mergers has hovered over me ever since my banking career began as a junior trainee at JP Morgan. Like Walter Shipley of Chase Manhattan at roughly the same time, I too was marked – or so I thought – by what is now known as a 'corporate event' which for a time shattered my intended career path.

Having set up my own bank consulting firm in large part to avoid such traumatic exogenous events, I have become increasingly fascinated by the theme of bank consolidation. Over the 1990s I have authored three reports for publication by our clients on European bank mergers. At the same time, the paradox explored in Chapter 1 has increasingly preoccupied me: if this is such a good thing to so many bankers and bank stockholders, why is there such an overwhelming body of evidence against its successful outcome?

The result has been another book, which essentially accumulates the off-the-record wisdom of people who have been through the process – in this case essentially senior bankers with extensive merger experience. We know only too well what the official position of their banks has been, and my hope is that the interview process will provide some deeper insights.

Our grateful thanks go first and foremost to our interviewees – those from the 33 banks interviewed as well as the many consultants and analysts who gave generously of their time and advice. Particular thanks go to McKinsey & Co. who were kind enough to permit the use of some of their presentational material.

While the purpose of the book is to let these merger veterans speak for themselves, I had to address early on the role of the narrator: was it to be 'I' the author, or, as I quickly resolved, the editorial 'we'? That decision led directly to the dedication of the book cited above. My colleagues at Davis International Banking Consultants, in particular Patrick Frazer, Diane Tovey and Dolores Mulroy, have truly made the book possible – partly for their contribution to the arguments made and data gathered, but also because writing it inevitably took time from the firm's consulting activities. Dolores Mulroy deserves a particular vote of thanks for converting indecipherable drafts into a finished product!

And a final word of appreciation to Stephen Rutt and his colleagues at the publishers who have picked up the challenge since the retirement of my good friend and former editor Tim Farmiloe.

London, December 1999   STEVEN I. DAVIS

Postscript

Proof-reading the text roughly six months after writing the original typescript provides confirmation of the speed at which the merger wave is transforming the banking world – both structurally and in human terms.

Thus within our universe alone a number of mergers have been announced since December: Unibank with MeritaNordbanken and Argentaria with BBV. Banco Comercial Portugues continues to buy smaller banks in its efforts to become a national champion in Portugal, while Bank of Tokyo Mitsubishi has responded to the merger mania of its peers with a similar merger. Arguably the most significant development has been the aborted bid by Deutsche Bank to combine with Dresdner Bank and the insurer Allianz in a pathfinding restructuring of the German financial sector.

And at the human level interviewees like Rudi Bogni have left the scene due to internal restructurings.

Rather than confuse the reader and delay publication by updating the text, however, we have left it untouched – but with this prefatory warning of the pace of change in the banking world.

London, May 2000   STEVEN I. DAVIS

1 The Bank Merger Paradox

As the new millennium opens, no issue has preoccupied bank management more than their role in the merger consolidation process. From Japan to Europe and the US, the merger wave has engulfed banks of every description. Table 1.1 provides a statistical profile of the value of such mergers since 1991.

In both the US and the Euro-area, which between them account for over 85 percent of the global total, the value of deals has accelerated since 1993/94. For each two-year period since then, the volume has more than doubled.

One result is an increase in concentration in many national markets. In the US, as indicated by Figure 1.1, a steady annual pace of about 500 mergers has reduced the number of banks from over 13,000 to less than 9,000 over the past decade. The largest US bank, Bank of America, now boasts an 8 per cent market share.

Driving this transformation has been a host of factors which are repeated across geographies. In countless management presentations and industry publications, they have been drummed into the minds of all participants in the banking game. At the risk of boring the reader with their repetition, we summarise them briefly below:

- *overcapacity*: By virtually any standard – capital requirements established by the Basle Committee, fierce price competition reflected in lower lending margins, the duplication of branch networks, etc. – overcapacity exists in all developed banking markets. More importantly, there is no obvious means of reducing or eliminating

Table 1.1 Value of banking M & A transactions accelerates (amounts in billions of dollars)

	US		Euro-area		Total	
	Amount	% increase	Amount	% increase	Amount	% increase
1991/92	56.8	NA	17.5	NA	84.7	NA
93/94	55.3	(2.6)	14.6	(1.7)	83.2	(1.2)
95/96	114.9	107.8	19.1	30.8	200.8	141.3
97/98	362.4	215.4	100.4	425.7	534.2	166.0

Sources: Bank for International Settlements; Securities Data Corp.

Figure 1.1 Sustained merger trend drives consolidation in US banking

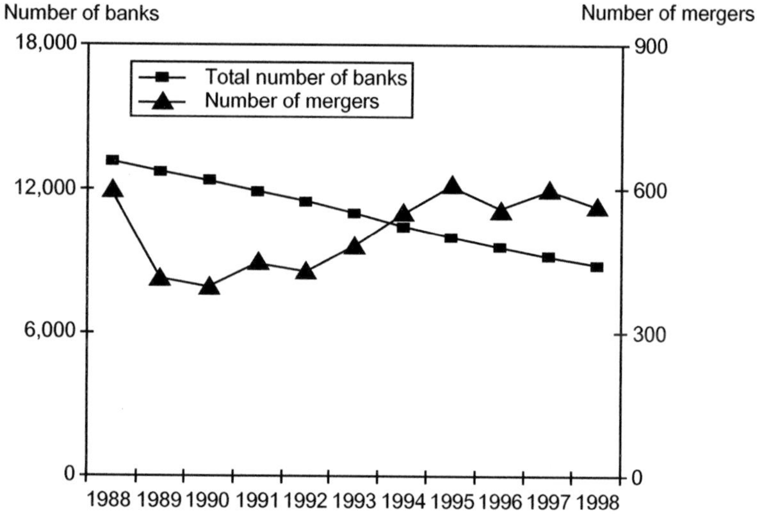

Source: Federal Deposit Insurance Corporation.

this surplus as bank consolidation in itself does not diminish the
sector's level of regulatory capital.

- *global competition*: Globalisation is a codeword in banking for the
  ability of a competitor from virtually any other market to enter
  another banking segment, often with a value proposition significantly superior to those of the established institutions. It also refers to
  the need to provide a global – and therefore expensive – service to
  clients who demand it.
- *deregulation*: While many banking markets have been effectively
  deregulated for years, the drumbeat continues: development of interstate banking and the effective repeal of the Glass–Steagall Act in
  the US, a 'Big Bang' in Japan, and the opening up of Singapore and
  other Asian markets to foreign banks. Such deregulation has fuelled
  the competitive fires described above and added to the industry's
  overcapacity, as non-bank financial institutions in particular offer
  banking products.
- *technology*: This codeword for electronic delivery of banking products – in particular the Internet – has undermined the banks'
  previous effective monopoly of payment systems as well as the
  profitability of traditional deposit and lending products. Lower-
  cost competitors have forced banks to slash their cost base and

meet this competition with their own direct offerings – largely to the benefit of the consumer.

During the 1990s, as the merger wave gained momentum, some new ingredients were added to the cocktail.

First, the phrase 'stockholder value' has entered the banker's vocabulary. Driven by the surge in ownership of bank stocks throughout the world by a handful of major fund managers based largely in the US, it is reflected in the demand by these institutions that bank management build their strategies around increasing their stock price. With 30–40 per cent of their stock now typically held by such demanding investors, banks in markets like Europe who had enjoyed relatively quiescent stockholders now respond briskly to such dictates – at the risk of a plummeting stock price which could attract predators or derail their own acquisition programme.

Supporting the stockholder value argument has been the apparent ability to demonstrate substantial savings on a discounted cash flow basis by a number of banks who have successfully executed in-market mergers. In Chapter 3 we explore in more detail these savings.

Secondly, a corollary to the emergence of stockholder value is the central role now played by relative market capitalisation. Historically banks have ranked themselves by asset size, with the relative importance of Tier 1 regulatory capital starting to play a role in the early 1990s following the 1988 Basle accord on capital adequacy. By the late 1990s, however, investment banking advisors were able to demonstrate that a higher market capitalisation not only offered more protection from predators but also the offensive ability to choose from a wider range of acquisition or merger options. A sharp debate on the value of size itself has ensued, but whatever its demerits the size of market capitalisation is a vital arrow in the quiver of bank management as it plots its strategic direction.

Finally, the personal agendas of many bank executives have increasingly dominated their bank's strategies. In any business one finds a number of chief executives attracted by the vision of market dominance and equipped with the energy and skills to achieve it. But the prospect of an 'end game' in banking, with a rapidly diminishing number of acceptable acquisition candidates to achieve that nirvana, has whetted the appetites of a growing number of bank CEOs. Making full use of the arguments for consolidation described above as well as a supportive market environment, so-called 'serial acquirers' have dominated the scene in the US and many European markets.

A remarkable consensus has therefore been achieved to the effect that the merger wave is not only inevitable but also, in many respects, a good thing. Bank staff unions, governments and even competition authorities in a surprisingly wide range of national markets accept its inevitability. For many participants and observers, the phrase 'end game' is widely used, with debate centring on the number and type of banks left standing when the merger wave is completed.

A sample of quotations from bank executives and their advisors gives a flavour of the environment:

- The name of the game is market share, market share, market share, and the only way to gain market share is through acquisition.[1]
- There are only so many premier franchises left; if you miss [one], you miss it forever.[2]
- The national [US] end game is closer than it may seem... The next five years [from 1997] will make the past five look tame.[3]

Yet these overwhelming arguments for bank mergers clash with equally convincing ones against consolidation from the academic, analyst and consulting communities.

Perhaps the most compelling arguments are expressed by academics and analysts who have examined the statistics for European and US mergers and concluded that, at best, the evidence for and against bank mergers is not conclusive. The majority view is that a large number of such mergers actually destroy stockholder value. While most studies focus on US bank mergers, several recent studies of European consolidation reinforce the US analysis.

Exhaustive analytical studies of key data pre- and post-merger such as returns on equity, cost/income ratios, and stock market performance reach essentially negative conclusions. Consider the following:

- A Wharton School study in 1996 of the vast existing literature to date concludes that:

    The value gains that are alleged to accrue... have not been verified ... gains by many measures are either small or non-existent... the results obtained are overwhelmingly unsupportive of the value effects. Both accounting and event studies offer no evidence of value gains. The average merger either has no effect on total firm value, or a slightly negative one.[4]

- A Bank for International Settlements study in August 1999 found that:

  Studies continue to indicate that the experience of a majority of [bank] mergers is disappointing, as organisational problems are systematically underestimated and acquirers tend to overpay for targets.[5]

- A study of North American bank mergers by the consulting firm Mitchell Madison in 1998 concludes that:

  The majority of the 1990–95 bank mergers were at best a wash and at worst a keen disappointment, an apparent triumph of managerial adrenaline over management intelligence.[6]

- A report by the Federal Reserve Bank of New York in 1997 summarises its findings as follows:

  We find no evidence to support the theory that in-market mergers lead to significant improvements in efficiency.[7]

- A book published in 1998 on bank mergers by the Stern School of Business summarises its findings as follows:

  Gains by many measures are either small or non-existent … the average merger has either no effect on total firm value, or a slightly negative one.[8]

Anecdotal evidence from specific transactions fuels these negative views. In the US, two signal examples of failed execution by previously successful serial acquirers – that of the old Wells Fargo/First Interstate and First Union/Core States deals – hammered the acquirers' reputation and stock price to the extent that Wells shortly succumbed itself to a take-over bid. Market pricing has clearly favoured the seller's stockholders with little left over for the buyer. Finally, projected future savings and synergies are reflected immediately in the market price with apparently little account taken of possible negative events.

Explanations for this apparent paradox abound. We shall examine in subsequent chapters the explanations offered by other analysts, academics and consultants.

The purpose of this volume is to fill the gap represented by the experience of senior bankers who have passed through the merger process and are prepared to express these views. The great majority of the publicly expressed views of their banks understandably support the positive dimension of merger results. By digging more deeply into the key drivers of successful execution of bank mergers, however, we might be able to cast some light on the disconnect between theory and practice. However the future consolidation pattern unfolds, these insights should be of use to both practitioners and their advisors.

We therefore approached senior executives in a number of banks in the US, Europe and Japan which have had extensive experience in implementing mergers during the decade of the 1990s. This time period covers both the great bulk of major mergers as well as the career experience of these executives. We have defined 'bank' to include essentially organisations which carry out as a core business the traditional banking functions of deposit taking and lending. Our candidates thus include, depending on the local nomenclature, retail and commercial banks as well as universal banking institutions. As interpenetration of the financial services sector continues, inevitably we shall encounter mergers involving the insurance, investment banking and other sectors, but our central focus is on these commercial banks.

The definition of 'merger' for our purposes includes essentially transactions which transform the merging entities in terms of culture, business mix, geography or another key dimension. We focus on mergers where the size differential is relatively small – in particular the categories of megamergers or 'mergers of equals' which generally pose the most significant execution risk. Our universe covers both in-market and out-of-market mergers as well as those complementary transactions in which a commercial bank acquires an investment banking or other non-traditional capability.

The response to our request for help was almost universally positive. Executives of a total of 33 banks were formally interviewed, and only a handful of those approached were unwilling to participate in the project. Our interviewees include six CEOs of merged banks. Other executives interviewed were senior managers – generally a member of the top management team – familiar with their merger experience. The ground-rules for each interview encouraged frankness by promising that comments would be provided on an off-the-record basis with actual attribution to individuals based on their express permission. Each interview began with the generic question 'What have been the lessons of your merger experience', followed by a series of questions directed at specific issues in the merger process, and concluding with the interviewee's view of the future.

We are particularly pleased that our coverage includes not only most of those banks widely associated with merger activity but also a broad geographic mix. Not only have we covered most of the banks who have led the US bank merger movement, but in Europe we have interviewed banks in the UK, France, Germany, Switzerland, Spain, Portugal, Italy, the Benelux region and Scandinavia. In Japan we interviewed the management of one of the early merger pairings, which in 1999 was replicated by a number of others.

For background information we have profiled these 33 institutions in the Appendix. In each case, we provide a general profile of the bank as well as more detailed comments on a recent (during the 1990s) major merger transaction. For each of the latter we detail the strategic objectives of the transaction as well as any specific financial targets established.

In our interviews, we focused on a number of issues which we felt would be of most value to the various readership constituencies involved:

- *banks* anxious to improve their future merger performance based on the experience of their peers
- *investors* struggling to differentiate merger winners from losers
- *analysts and consultants* hoping to glean some useful lessons from actual merger experience

In this context, the issues of most interest to us are the following:

- Can we draw any conclusions on the extent to which the mergers in question have achieved their objectives?
- What behaviour characterises winning and losing merger strategies?
- What are the critical factors behind the success of the most admired merger practitioners?
- How do successful merging banks address such critical issues as merger preparation, due diligence, the choice of key executives and IT systems, cultural change and the retention of key staff and clients?
- How can an outside observer evaluate the likely success of specific transactions?
- How might the future merger pattern evolve based on the experience of these banks and environmental factors?

Our approach thus has not been to obtain views on whether a given merger in retrospect was good or bad in concept. Rather our focus is on execution: once the deal had been decided in principle and the price and other parameters agreed, what lessons did management glean from its subsequent execution and implementation? While we do not address the validity of the original decision, we shall opine on the possible shape of future merger decisions by addressing the last of these six issues in our concluding chapter.

We have made a particular effort to profile, in the form of case studies in the body of the text, eight cases which we find particularly useful in terms of the lessons learned. In each of our interviews we asked for names of merger pairings which were viewed as particularly successful as well as those which provided more negative lessons. The results of this straw poll are provided in Chapter 11.

In addition to these interviews which form the core of our intellectual contribution, we have dug deeply into the existing literature on bank mergers as well as interviewed over a dozen non-bank sources of insight to test our findings – again on an off-the-record basis. Our desk research focused on the findings and conclusions of the work of others, and we did not attempt to replicate the statistical analysis carried out so comprehensively by so many competent academics and analysts.

In our interview series conducted with bank consultants and analysts, we were able to talk confidentially with most of the major management and IT consulting firms with active banking practices, and we quote liberally from them in subsequent chapters. We were somewhat less successful in gleaning the views of many leading bank analysts on the 'Street', who may well have been reluctant to contradict the positive view they express publicly on the merger process.

We also validated the views of our bank interviewees by off-the-record conversations with many friends who were former colleagues in the merging banks and who might have a different opinion of the success of their merger process. Inevitably these views might reflect the circumstances of their departure, but they are included to provide some balance of evidence.

One other caveat: this book is not designed as a 'how-to-do-it' manual for future bank pairings. The post-merger integration practices of leading consulting firms are impressive by any standard: breadth of experience, knowledge of the key technical and human dimensions, and accumulation of an experiential data base. We have injected in our text a number of tables and charts from the material kindly made available by several of these firms – primarily to provide texture and substance to the merger issues raised.

The chapters which follow move from the strategic to the implementation phases and back to the strategic as we provide our own findings and conclusions. Chapters 2 through 9 and Chapter 12 essentially reflect the views expressed by our interviewees, while the report card in Chapter 10, case studies in Chapter 11 and concluding Chapter 13 provide our own.

Thus Chapter 2 examines the strategic views which underpin the mergers under study. We characterise the projected strategic objectives – size, market share, strategic positioning, offensive – as those adding to future stockholder value but not easily quantifiable. Chapter 3 then looks at specific financial targets – essentially cost savings – which most market observers regard as the principal means of achieving true stockholder value. Our analysis of the execution phase of the merger begins with Chapter 4, which examines the lessons of merger preparation – essentially the decisions made, during the first few months, following agreement on the financial terms of the transaction. They include the structure and strategy of the new institution, the selection of key executives, key merger processes and time frame, and selection of major IT systems.

Chapter 5 addresses the lessons learned from due diligence – that preliminary phase of the merger process which should enable the respective parties to identify major potential problems such as asset quality, systems adequacy, the capabilities of key executives. In Chapter 6 we discuss the role of leadership and the form it takes in our banking universe. This is followed in Chapter 7 by the issues of selection and motivation of key personnel. Chapter 8 addresses the universal issue of cultural conflict and the means used to address the problem. Our analytical chapters conclude with Chapter 9, which evaluates the selection and conversion of IT systems. Chapter 10 summarises our view of the relative success of our universe in achieving its merger goals, with particular reference to financial targets.

In Chapter 11 we analyse eight case studies of past mergers which, in our view and that of the participants in our straw poll, offer particularly useful lessons for the future. The views of our interviewees on the outlook for the future are profiled in Chapter 12. Finally, in Chapter 13 we conclude with our own thoughts on the key issues raised by our analysis as well as our vision of the future.

2 Strategic Positioning: The Passion for Scale and Scope

Our definition of strategic positioning includes an array of objectives designed to provide long-term competitive advantage.

When seeking enlightenment on the value of these objectives from company documents such as prospectuses, press releases and road show presentations, the strategic analyst is met with a bewildering array of verbiage. The phrases 'critical mass', 'European scale', 'bank of the regions', 'national champion', 'global player', 'multi-niche', 'super-regional bank' and others trip lightly off the tongue of bank managements from Tokyo to Toronto to Turin. While much of this verbiage is deliberately designed to obfuscate, the concept of strategic positioning itself defies quantification.

The analyst must thus dig more deeply. When he does, a number of more sharply defined objectives usually emerge. In most of the banks profiled in the Appendix and interviewed for this book, there is more than one strategic objective. They can be summarised as follows:

- *size*: Few banks will acknowledge that size (or scale) alone drives their merger strategy, but it is an inevitable consequence of any merger. Size and scale are often used connote physical attributes, although some analysts use 'scale' to refer to size within a given market segment. Physical size has traditionally been a measure of banking achievement. In the 1990s, as we mentioned above, it was reinforced by the central importance of market capitalisation as a vehicle for expansion. Inherent in bulking up in size is the defensive argument: a larger bank is likely to have fewer possible predators.
- *market share*: Building market share is a natural strategic objective, particularly in a desirable business with attractive profit and growth potential. As in so many consolidating businesses, being a market leader brings advantages of pricing power, cost economies, insights into customer behaviour, and visibility to clients.
- *geographic expansion*: Entering new markets is an understandable motive, particularly for banks who have reached the practical limits of expansion in their home market, lured by the prospect of national

coverage in the US or the European single market, or attracted by an underdeveloped, 'emerging' market.

- *broadening the product range*: The argument of scope – essentially breadth of product offering – is a powerful one, particularly in a deregulating business where banking is being subsumed into the broader category of financial services. The siren song of cross-selling to an existing customer base has long been a compelling one, which we evaluate further in Chapter 3.
- *defensive*: While rarely cited publicly, the desire to retain one's independence, or at least relative autonomy, has driven a number of bank mergers. At one extreme are the 'white knight' responses to an unfriendly bid. At the other are pre-emptive strikes designed to fend off possible future attempts.

The rich tapestry of strategic motives of the banks interviewed defies simple categorisation or segmentation. One can, however, identify a number of patterns in the major developed banking markets. Of the 33 mergers profiled in the Appendix, 11, or one-third, either did not quantify the financial synergies to be obtained from the merger or targeted modest combined savings of a few percentage points. This chapter will focus on the strategic rationale of this segment as well as several which combined cost savings with a significant strategic transformation.

Most of the mergers profiled in this book aim strategically at building market share and scale to compete more effectively in a consolidating market. The relaxation of US interstate banking regulations has fuelled the aggressive expansion plans of banks such as Fleet Boston, First Union, Wells Fargo and Bank One.

The European counterpart of this surge in the 1990s has been the one–two punch of the formation of the Single European market in 1992 ('EU '92') and the introduction of the € in 1999. Each provoked successive waves of anticipatory in-market mergers in markets like Spain, the Nordic region, Benelux and Austria.

The delayed reaction to these global developments has finally reached Japan, where by the end of the decade the forces of deregulation and competition had unleashed a series of mega- mergers which at last may transform the competitive environment. Beginning in August 1999, no less than three major consolidations were announced during the year. The trio of Industrial Bank of Japan, Dai-Ichi Kangyo and Fuji Bank will create (at the time of announcement) the world's largest bank in asset terms, while Sumitomo Bank and Sakura Bank will unite to form the second largest. Tokai Bank and Asahi Bank will form a smaller 'multi-regional' bank, while other combinations among the country's major institutions are likely to follow. These announcements telescope into weeks a process which has taken years in the supposedly fast-moving banking sectors in the US and Europe. It has been driven by the same global factors plus a growing awareness in Japan that returns on capital must improve to attract equity funds for future growth.

We examine first, however, the mergers which offer primarily strategic benefits.

STRATEGIC POSITIONING WITHOUT MAJOR COST SAVES

In many European countries, the cost savings analysed in the next chapter are simply impossible to achieve given local labour regulations and the social environment. Several Belgian banks, for example, have structured their merger strategy accordingly. One of the most articulate in this respect is Dexia, the merger of Belgian and French municipal financiers. Paul Vanzeveren, one of the four members of Dexia's executive group, explains:

> Our goal is not to cut costs but to grow, in precisely defined terms, internationally and in our core markets of public finance and fund management. Cost synergies will be pursued where possible but are sometimes hard to achieve with the structural and regulatory rigidities in France and Belgium, but Dexia is still a catalyst for further integration. Size is important but not the essence. Creating size doesn't necessarily mean creating value. Too many mergers are driven by considerations of size, power and leadership. There's early optimism as people delude themselves, and the market is ultimately disappointed.

With cost savings marginal or non-existent, the model of complementary mergers has become well developed in Europe. In our survey of the 'Class of 1990' mergers – those triggered largely by the advent of the single European market in 1992 and profiled in Chapter 4 – this was clearly a favoured strategy.

The early *bancassurance* mergers bringing together major banks and insurers in the Benelux region have not only been replicated subsequently across Europe but also created financial giants whose market capitalisations dominate European league tables. Thus ING Group and Fortis are among the top 10 in Europe by market cap and have used their market clout to acquire other financial institutions as well as begin to generate significant cost economies from the resulting mix. As Henjo Hielkema, Vice Chairman of Fortis and one of its four top executives, puts it:

> We are consolidators.... We started with a modest banking presence [VSB] in Holland and discovered that this was nothing in a European or even Benelux context....we quickly looked for our next target [ASLK/CGER].... when ABN Amro decided to sell MeesPierson we jumped at it aggressively. In retrospect these were two great acquisitions – well timed and companies which flourished...We had just started discussing in 1997 how to integrate the three banks in a post-EMU environment when Suez appeared as a seller of Générale Bank. Now we've integrated them all on a line-of-business basis as Fortis Bank.

Its *bancassurance* peer in the Netherlands, ING Group, has followed a somewhat different strategic development: a federation of financial institutions in the US and Europe with a high degree of operating autonomy. Managing Board member Hessel Lindenbergh describes the philosophy:

> We have a preference for well-run institutions which can work together in a quiet and co-operative spirit. We have respect for each other. There's lots of value in maintaining local autonomy. Unless there's trouble (as in the case of Barings which was acquired from the Bank of England following its failure) we prefer to take time to get to know each other. If the various units (like Banque Bruxelles Lambert in Belgium and BHF in Germany) can work together and focus their energies on a specific project, it's very inspiring and motivating. It's impossible to walk in and take over. A federation takes more time but it's a more natural process.

Another practitioner of the complementary merger is BG Bank in Denmark, now part of Kapital Holding. An initial merger brought together the savings bank Bikuben with the payments specialist Giro-Bank. The two units have continued their separate development and been joined in Kapital Holding by Realkredit, a mortgage specialist which has maintained its operating identity – as well as selling most of its product outside the group. As Managing Board member Gert Kristensen explains, through the merger process,

> we've become a major player [against the two larger Danish banks] and been able to move on to the next step. We've shown we can succeed in taking advantage of corporate opportunities. With Realkredit, there are legal barriers to integration, and it's a problem, but we have integrated several central functions. There aren't as many savings as the investors would like, but that's the nature of a complementary business.

A second wave of European consolidation in the late 1990s has taken the form of the acquisition of insurers by major national banks. Designed to boost the latters' presence in the fund management sector as well as bulk up market capitalisation and tap new retail distribution channels, banks such as Credit Suisse, Skandinaviska Enskilda Banken, Unibank, Den Danske Bank and Den norske Bank have all acquired smaller life and non-life insurers in their home market. In each of these, projected cost savings have been modest.

The synergistic results have been mixed. Tom Grondahl, a member of the top management team of Den norske Bank, which acquired the Vital Insurance group, explains:

> It's difficult to mix the two cultures, and even tougher if there are legal barriers. We own the stock of Vital but its Board is also responsible to the policy holders, and there's a natural conflict in as much as our earnings are to be shared between stockholders and policyholders. The Ministry of Finance has said that Vital must be an independent entity within a new holding company.

Another fascinating variant of the *bancassurance* model from the prolific and creative Benelux banking community has been the formation of KBC Banking and Insurance. A three-way merger of Flemish-based banks and insurers, it was designed essentially as a defensive measure to ensure their continued independence as well as providing the capital base to expand into other markets. Ignace Temmerman, Managing Director of KBC's subsidiary bank CBC, describes the philosophy:

> The dominant stockholder, Almanij, wanted to avoid being marginalised as well as remain independent. We explored several alternative

strategies but finally decided on a Belgian merger. We have maintained a Flemish anchorage!

In the rapidly consolidating Italian market, the federal model has taken another form. A handful of leading banks is acquiring control of mid-sized institutions, retaining brand names and local autonomy but often centralising core systems, product manufacture and control functions. UniCredito, Italy's largest bank in terms of market capitalisation, is a skilled practitioner of this strategy. Roberto Nicastro, head of planning and control, describes the process:

> The key is to be flexible. In some cases, such as a superior performing bank, you don't want to exercise detailed control so you accept for some time not occupying the driver's seat. In other cases, you may have lots of debate with the sellers, but in the end you have to do the deal if you can warrant some minimum conditions for exercising adequate governance and direction – it's a no brainer. We then focus on performance targets to help people get their act together.

In Germany, the *landesbanken* – large institutions owned by regional public sector entities but operating largely in the commercial marketplace – have presented a unique merger profile. While most are essentially wholesale banks with marginal profitability, there are two recent cases – Bankgesellschaft Berlin (BGB) and Landesbank Baden – Wuerttemberg (LBBW) – where profitable retail elements have been merged with such wholesale banks to create what could become highly profitable investment vehicles. Sadly, the dominant influence of political factors has hampered their development. As a former executive of BGB puts it:

> It's a great concept – the umbrella organisation – the only way the landesbanks can solve the Brussels problem (the debate over subsidised cost of funds for the banks). But they've become a political animal. The cultural clashes are horrendous, and strategic issues haven't been addressed. It's all about appearances and the testosterone of politicians.

His pessimism is echoed by an insider at LBBW:

> It's all driven by politics. They talk about targets, not facts. They don't think that way. Getting bigger and more international is

the goal. Bringing together the various political interests and agreeing the ownership breakdown was a major achievement. To have tried to agree in advance on strategy might have killed the whole process.

A classic complementary merger was Credit Agricole's acquisition of Banque Indosuez in France. Having difficulty in building rapidly its international and investment banking capability on an organic basis, France's largest bank jumped at the chance to acquire Indosuez from the Suez group. Bernard Michel, Deputy Managing Director of Credit Agricole who managed the process, explains:

> We were perfectly clear about our objectives: to accelerate our international development and build a world-wide capital markets capability. Unlike a lot of banks who simply want to get bigger – perhaps to protect themselves – we had a clear industrial logic.

As in so many other dimensions, the Japanese strategic model is unique. The widely accepted need for banking consolidation has met a hitherto irresistible barrier: cultural resistance to change – not to speak of cost reduction through forced redundancies. The complementary merger in 1996 to create what was then Japan's largest bank, Bank of Tokyo Mitsubishi (BTM), is now being replicated by a host of others designed to address the ills of the banking system. A friend at BTM describes the issues they must face:

> We haven't done much restructuring yet – just merged overseas branches of the two banks in the same location. It took Dai Ichi Kangyo [DKB] 20 years to make major changes after their merger, and it's taken us three, so that's progress! We've got to move faster in the future, and the process has started. But it won't be brutal. It will be a Japanese model. Letting people go will not be a priority.

COMBINED POSITIONING AND SYNERGIES

In the United States, the strategic dimension of bank mergers has been driven largely by the relaxation of interstate banking regulations beginning in 1994 and the resulting explosion of 'out-of-market' deals. A new phrase, 'geographic footprint', has entered the banker's vocabulary as the most aggressive competitors drive for the national coverage attained decades ago in virtually all other banking markets.

Unlike the case in Europe and Japan, however, virtually all of these mergers involve a significant element of cost saves, generally from reduction in head office costs in the acquired bank but also from the closure of overlapping branches. We profile the merger strategies of four of these banks – Fleet Boston, First Union, Bank One and Wells Fargo – in the Appendix. Apart from the cost synergies discussed in the next chapter, the strategic rationale rests on the need for scale to invest in common technology platforms and achieve market share in attractive geographies. Ken Lewis, who runs the retail business of the new Bank of America, now America's largest bank with an 8 per cent market share, is quoted as saying:

> I cannot overemphasize the importance of scale and size in today's environment.[1]

A new model for strategic mergers, however, was introduced in the US by the 1998 fusion between Citibank and the Travelers Insurance group. Designed primarily to increase revenues by cross-selling retail and wholesale financial products within the group, the Citigroup transaction has attracted widespread interest, particularly from the array of banks threatened by slowing revenue growth. The Citigroup merger is the only one of the US mergers reviewed in this book which did not target quantified synergies. Citigroup's Jack Morris, its public affairs director and public spokesman for the merger, explains the approach:

> It's very early days – very much a work in progress – but the evidence so far is that the business proposition is unassailable. We've not tried to project the value added from the merger, but there's enormous potential. For example, retail Citibankers have largely been order takers until now, and we're trying to export Travelers' financial planning model to the branch network.

In Europe, several mergers have aimed at transforming the participating banks as well as generating significant cost savings. Thus Deutsche Bank in 1999 spent the equivalent of one-third of its market capitalisation to acquire Bankers Trust Company in order to gain strength in key investment and corporate banking segments as well as penetrate the US market. For members of the management team who would have preferred a German or European-based strategy, this was traumatic. Leaving the execution of the merger to Anglo-Saxon professionals only doubled the pain.

Another transforming merger is that of MeritaNordbanken. The first true cross-border merger of equals of major banks, this brought together the largest Finnish and fourth largest Swedish bank to create what will hopefully become the first true Nordic financial institution with roots in each of the four markets. While some cost synergies are projected, the challenge is daunting. As Ari Laakso, head of administration in Helsinki and a veteran of a series of mergers in Finland, points out:

> We've merged in Finland every two to three years, and trying to do normal business and merge at the same time takes a lot out of you! Now we have the issue of Finland vs. Sweden – it's a relationship which has never been easy, as we've always been competitors. It's a multi-cultural, multi-market challenge – not an easy management job. MeritaNordbanken has very little to do with either Nordbanken or Merita – it's a wholly new company. And when we become three or four banks, it will be a brand new game again.

Finally, the 1997 merger of two of the three major Swiss banks into UBS AG combined both defensive and offensive strategic motives. Fusing two European-based investment banking entities created a more powerful competitor for the US-based leaders, while merging two marginally profitable domestic retail branch networks should significantly boost combined earnings. Marcel Ospel, the group's CEO, also muses about what might have happened had he not taken the initiative to merge SBC and the old UBS:

> In the two years since we merged, the same forces driving consolidation are at work – and are even stronger. There's a paradigm shift with a period of dramatic crowding out beginning in 2002, and I really don't know what will be the story in four years. But whatever the outcome, we can say that something would have happened to SBC or UBS or both if we had not merged!

The panorama of strategic objectives profiled above poses a number of issues. First, are these the right strategic moves? Does it make sense to deploy scarce resources in highly competitive markets such as global investment banking, the manufacture of the fund management or insurance product, or a neighbouring banking market? Is it likely that stockholder value will be maximised on the new capital at management's disposition?

Secondly, can these initiatives be successfully executed? Is the resulting entity so large and complex that it becomes unwieldy, while investors complain of a conglomerate which should in financial logic be broken up?

We shall address these and other issues in Chapter 13.

3 Cost and Revenue Synergies: The Basis for Increasing Stockholder Value

While higher revenues are often projected in merger documents, it is cost savings which generally underpin the stockholder value calculations made by investors in evaluating bank mergers.

The clear consensus of the bank analysts and institutional investors we interviewed is to estimate the value added by calculating the present value of future savings based on management's projections and discounting them at an appropriate rate of interest. As we discuss below, revenue synergies are usually viewed as an extra benefit but far less reliable than cost savings. It is this net present value which can then be related to other investment alternatives and evaluated against market values. For the analyst, such cost saves constitute a benchmark against which management will be measured. Increasingly, cost savings are reported net of estimated revenue losses.

THE US COST-SAVING MODEL

This model has been shaped and refined in the US, where estimated cost savings have been both substantial and well publicised. For the reasons indicated in Chapter 2, it has been translated with some difficulty into other markets such as Europe. Yet it continues to drive both investor perceptions as well as much management behaviour.

The rationale for cost savings in the current and likely future banking environment is well articulated by John Skerritt, the head of Andersen Consulting's global financial institutions practice:

> The goal is to drive excess capacity out of the market. There's too much duplicated IT and other investments which can't be sustained given the new, low-cost distribution channels. Consumers are driving the whole business, and we need to jettison as much of the acquired infrastructure as possible!

20

He is echoed by Brian Moynihan, SVP and responsible for merger integration of Fleet Boston, one of the most successful and active serial acquirers in the US:

> We're driven by economics. Customers won't allow current high product prices with lower cost alternatives available. We've got to cut costs. We're going to continue to live in this tough competitive environment. Our merger model therefore is to convert to our platform, cut out duplicated overhead, and knock out excess management layers.

With hundreds of bank mergers taking place each year, the US has understandably developed the most refined merger cost model. As indicated by Figure 3.1, the principal sources of cost savings are central

Figure 3.1 Likely source of merger cost savings

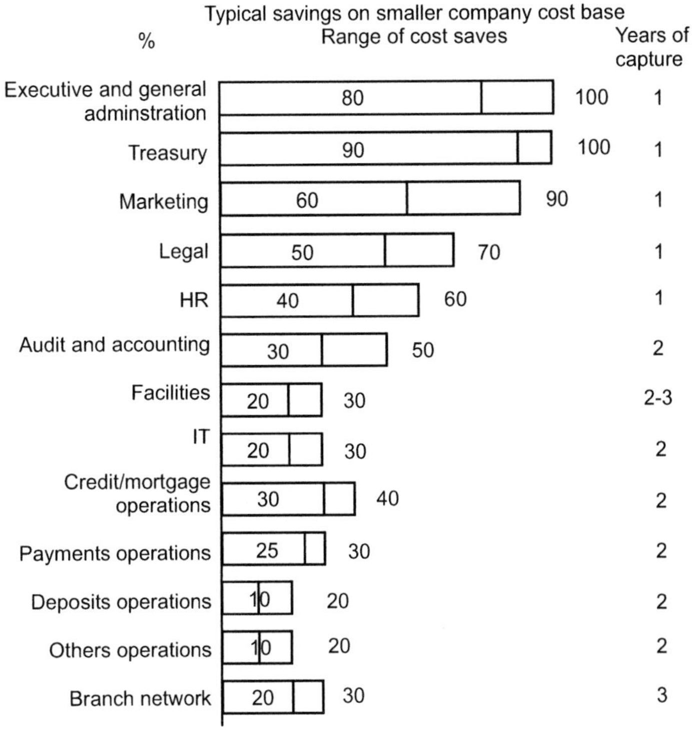

%	Typical savings on smaller company cost base Range of cost saves		Years of capture
Executive and general adminstration	80	100	1
Treasury	90	100	1
Marketing	60	90	1
Legal	50	70	1
HR	40	60	1
Audit and accounting	30	50	2
Facilities	20	30	2-3
IT	20	30	2
Credit/mortgage operations	30	40	2
Payments operations	25	30	2
Deposits operations	10	20	2
Others operations	10	20	2
Branch network	20	30	3

Source: McKinsey & Company.

functions and the branch network. Closing down a smaller bank's headquarters, merging dealing rooms, and combining central functions such as marketing, personnel, audit and legal staffs can slash from 50–100 per cent of the smaller bank's relevant cost base. Equally important is the ability to achieve such savings within the first year of the merger period.

Only 20–30 per cent of branch costs are likely to be saved when overlapping units are shuttered. Since about two-thirds of a typical retail bank's cost base is located in the branch network, however, closing duplicated branch networks also represents major potential savings. The challenge, as we shall discuss below, is to retain all but a small percentage of the clients who are asked to switch branches.

Figure 3.2 portrays the planned or achieved reduction in number of branches in a selection of recent US and European mergers. Most reductions for such in-market mergers are grouped around the average of 23 per cent.

Figure 3.2   Planned/achieved branch reduction from selected in-market mergers

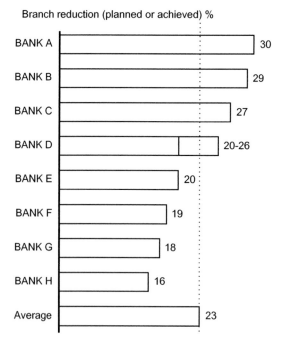

Branch reduction (planned or achieved) %

BANK A	30
BANK B	29
BANK C	27
BANK D	20-26
BANK E	20
BANK F	19
BANK G	18
BANK H	16
Average	23

Source: McKinsey & Company.

Figure 3.3 In-market vs. out-of-market cost savings

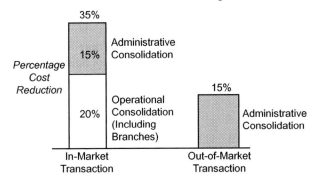

Source: Corporate Advisory Board, First Manhattan Consulting Group.

As indicated by Figure 3.3, pure in-market mergers (with total overlap of branch networks) can normally achieve cost savings in the range of 30–40 per cent of the target, or smaller, bank's total cost base. As branch overlap diminishes, so do the aggregate potential savings, with the result that the US rule of thumb for an 'out-of-market' merger is roughly 15 per cent of the smaller bank's costs – essentially closing down its central functions.

Undisclosed but significant cost savings often underpin aggregate performance targets. As indicated in Chapter 2, about a third of the banks interviewed do not publicise cost reduction targets. For many of these banks, however, cost savings are a significant element of the merger strategy. Reasons for not publicly acknowledging cost targets vary from reluctance to being held by the market to targets which ultimately might not be met, to the avoidance of adverse publicity in the local community and with labour unions.

Particularly in a European environment, advertising massive redundancies is seen by many as an unnecessary hostage to fortune. Thus Kent Atkinson, Lloyds TSB's Chief Financial Officer, prefers to promise aggregate cost saves from the TSB merger without providing more detail:

We don't publish branch or staff reduction targets, even though we've already closed 600 branches since the merger. It doesn't serve any purpose except that of the unions, and it unsettles staff and customers. I can't understand why some of our competitors do it!

Achieving these savings requires one-off restructuring costs, which are generally booked at the time of the merger. In the US and many

European markets, these approximate one to two times the projected annual savings. In our European interview series, however, we were told of much higher cost/benefit ratios stemming from the need to pay handsome 'voluntary' retirement benefits, particularly for senior staff in markets with strong union influence. One Spanish banker thus told us of paying up redundancy costs of to five times salary in a recent negotiation, while an Austrian bank executive estimated the cost/benefit ratio in his market at 3:1.

EXPORTING THE US MODEL

US bank analysts often have great difficulty grasping the institutional constraints on many Continental banks' ability to reduce costs and improve productivity. In markets like Spain, France, Austria and Belgium, long-standing binding agreements with staff and other unions set out salary scales, job descriptions and working conditions in extraordinary detail.

To move staff physically, for example, from the branch to a call centre or central processing unit, much less giving them early retirement, requires a negotiated agreement with unions who often command considerable political support at the highest levels. Thus in France, for example, a 50-year-old agreement dating from the early post-war years continues in force. When Société Générale in the mid-1990s bought the smaller bank Crédit du Nord, it was thus obliged to retain the framework agreement applicable to Crédit du Nord's employees.

Across Europe, management frequently make public commitments that their merger in itself will not result in forced redundancies. As many of our banks confirmed, the merger would not have occurred without this commitment.

Figure 3.4 provides a rough estimate of the typical breakdown of such restructuring costs. Severance pay accounts for about half of the total, with incremental IT integration and network restructuring expenses representing about 20 per cent each.

In management's discounted cash flow calculations, the time frame for restructuring costs and savings is clearly of central importance. Savings in the branch network are highly dependent on completion of the necessary conversion to the chosen retail banking system, which usually constitutes the end of the merger period and the date at which full merger savings start to be realised.

Our interviews in the US indicated that an 18–24 month merger period is typical. In Europe, as indicated in the profiles in the

Figure 3.4 Costs and benefits of merger restructuring

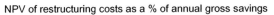

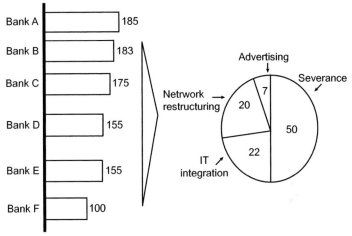

Source: McKinsey & Company.

Appendix, the merger period can run to four years and longer, as a new retail banking platform may have to be built to replace existing dated legacy systems. In addition, in many European countries, staff reduction takes place through attrition and current hiring freezes, in line with commitments made to facilitate the merger.

The wave of Japanese bank mergers announced in 1999 adopts a uniquely Japanese approach to cost savings. Forecasts submitted in 1999 to the government in connection with the receipt of public funds indicated cost reduction programmes of roughly 10 per cent over the period to 2003 to generate overall returns on equity in the region of 6 per cent. Arguably the subsequent spate of mega-mergers stems from an awareness that such returns are inadequate in a competitive market for bank capital.

In practice, the reaction of most leading Japanese banks to cost reduction is similar to that of many continental European peers. Thus attrition of the work force, combined technology investment, leverage with vendors, and improved work practices – rather than massive redundancies – are likely to characterise future cost reduction programmes. As our friend at Bank of Tokyo Mitsubishi says:

> We've learned a lot from studying banks like Chase and Deutsche Bank. The process has started. But it can be a very slow process in a very big bank.

While the overall profile of bank costs is probably quite similar in all major banking markets, there is a spirited debate over whether European banks, for example, can achieve the same level of savings as their US peers. Figures 3.5 and 3.6 would indicate little difference in aggregate projected savings for a range of mergers with considerable overlap. In fact, some of the most substantial relative savings – UBS/SBC and Bank Austria/Creditanstalt – have been projected in Europe. In both markets, relatively modest single-digit savings have been projected for complementary transactions or those with a minor degree of geographic overlap.

Several of the European bankers interviewed strongly affirm that the cost-saving potential is roughly equivalent. Luis Bastida, Chief Financial Officer of Banco Bilbao Vizcaya, points out that:

> It's only a question of time. In the US you can get 30 per cent savings in 18 months; in Spain you need three to five years. Fixed costs are only fixed in the long term.

Much depends on management's priorities, the profile of the bank and its cost base. Wells Fargo projects a relatively modest 8 per cent (for a US bank) net savings after the merger period because of its

Figure 3.5   American and Canadian banks: estimated cost savings as per cent of combined costs

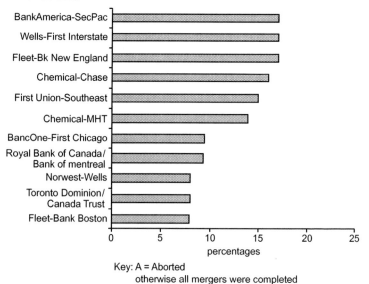

Key: A = Aborted
otherwise all mergers were completed

Source: DIBC research and company data.

Figure 3.6 European bank mergers: estimated cost savings as per cent of combined costs

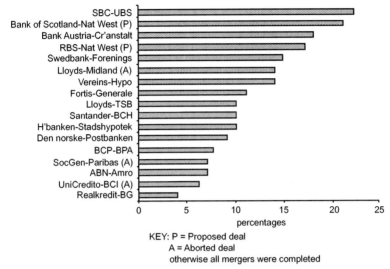

KEY: P = Proposed deal
A = Aborted deal
otherwise all mergers were completed

Source: DIBC research and company documents.

determination to build a new retail platform and to spend heavily on training and systems to enhance cross-selling. UBS has targeted an ambitious 23 per cent staff reduction, but much of this has taken place in the relatively flexible London and New York markets. As we shall discuss later, First Union attempted to achieve 40 per cent savings in its Core States acquisition over a tight 12-month time frame and succeeded in destroying the economics of the transaction.

For out-of-market deals – essentially cross border in Europe and complementary transactions such as bank/insurance linkages – the savings are understandably modest. Figure 3.7 profiles a selection of such out-of-market deals in Europe and the US. The Deutsche Bank/Bankers Trust transaction is projected to achieve a relatively high 10 per cent savings because of overlap in capital market operations.

The pressure to reduce costs to achieve profitability targets after the merger period has transformed the business strategies of a number of the banks interviewed. Banks such as Fortis, Argentaria and Bank One, which had espoused the federal model early in their merger evolution, have since moved to an integrated approach. Duplicated IT costs, parallel staff units and internal friction have driven such banks to

Bank Mergers

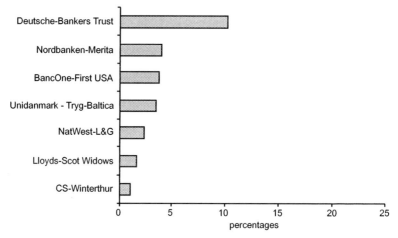

Source: DIBC research and company data.

abandon the merits of operating autonomy. As the Chief Financial Officer of one of these institutions acknowledges:

> The original federal model [of three separate retail networks] was very inefficient. Today the market is changing very fast, and more efficient banks can leave us behind. By integrating into a single bank we're more efficient and focused. But you need to be courageous to take the step.

While analysts debate the merits of being a 'serial acquirer', in the realm of cost reduction there is no doubt in the minds of the banks interviewed that merger experience pays off. Chase and Bank Austria are among those who have applied their initial experience – both positive and negative – with mega-mergers early in the decade to their most recent transaction. Thus General Manager Danilo Melamed of Bank Austria, who monitored the bank's earlier merger between Laenderbank and Z Bank, points out that:

> This time we're more clever. We don't make so many compromises. Top management is fully committed this time – they know how many times we compromised last time when some management board members said 'you can't cut that!'

At the new Chase Manhattan, Senior Country Officer Mark Garvin supervised in London both the original ManHan/Chemical as well as the Chase/Chemical merger. As he explains:

> We do a 'lessons' booklet after each merger and circulate it internally. I had all the old merger manuals on my shelf when we sat down to meet with our Chase colleagues.

The cost estimates tabled in offer documents and prospectuses may or may not reflect informed and detailed analysis of the likely cost reduction possibilities. In some cases they are assembled hurriedly in hotel rooms with the help of investment bankers who have little experience in bank operations. Thus the unfriendly bids in 1999 by the two Scottish banks for NatWest in the UK were underpinned by estimates derived from external analysis. And the consequences are serious: as one friend in a European bank acquired in an unfriendly merger points out:

> We haven't delivered yet on some cost estimates which were probably made by a bunch of investment bankers trying to justify a deal. There's a lot of stress!

The stress is truly overwhelming. Several of our interviewees who were present on the occasion describe graphically the pressure exerted on management and its consultants when the chief executive of a serial acquirer announces to all concerned that the market valuation of his deal will decline by perhaps $30–40 million for each month's delay in merger execution.

REVENUE SYNERGIES: THE TRIUMPH OF HOPE OVER EXPERIENCE?

Widespread scepticism exists over the ability of banks to generate revenue synergies through mergers. Most major banks already offer a full palette of retail and corporate banking products. In a highly competitive environment with an increasingly sophisticated client base, increased sales per client are likely to come from replacing an existing provider. As the author of a recent bank merger study puts it:

> Achieving revenue synergies requires decisions from powerful external constituents – the customer! Bank acquirors have massively

Figure 3.8 Projected revenue synergies as per cent of combined revenues

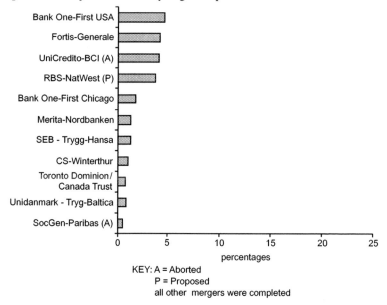

KEY: A = Aborted
P = Proposed
all other mergers were completed

Source: DIBC research and company documents.

underestimated the time and effort to develop and market a better (value) proposition.[1]

Tom Grondahl of DnB mentions another constraint emerging from his own merger experience:

The income synergies you think you will get might easily be lost because of unrest in the organisations after the merger.

Figure 3.8 provides a summary of the revenue synergies projected by a number of North American and European mergers. In no case do they exceed 5 per cent of the combined revenue base. In many instances, the bulk of these modest increments stem from the sale of non-life insurance products to be sold as part of a banking package. The largest synergies were projected for the merger of Bank One with its credit card acquisition First USA and by Fortis, who will apply the lessons of cross-selling success of one Belgian affiliate to another.

Yet a number of banks continue to win additional revenues from the merger process. Among the banks interviewed, Wells Fargo and Banco

Figure 3.9   Percentage of customer funds loss per branch closed

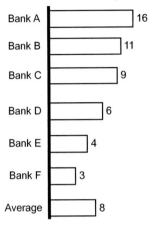

Source: McKinsey & Company.

Comercial Portugues (BCP) have a track record of improving the cross-sell ratio of the banks they acquire. As Pedro Libano Monteiro of BCP explains:

> For us, cross-selling is a question of survival. If we don't cross-sell, we're in trouble. In mutual funds, our ratio is roughly 30 per cent.

In Europe, where *bancassurance* (the sale of insurance to bank branch customers) evolved to a fine art during the 1990s, cross-selling experience has been mixed. As indicated above, Fortis anticipates substantial revenue gains from applying best practice in their Belgium savings bank ASLK to their new acquisition Générale Bank. On the other hand, in the UK, where the product and competitor profile is different, bank/insurance pairings like the failed NatWest/Legal & General linkage in 1999 have been widely criticised.

One of the challenging issues raised by the merger process is the relationship between cost savings and revenue losses. In the branch closure equation, there is clearly a link between the number and location of branches closed and the revenue losses from customers who go elsewhere. Figure 3.9 profiles the experience of one consulting firm in this key equation.

CLIENT RETENTION: A CRITICAL FACTOR IN THE MERGER CALCULUS

The issue of customer retention in general is a key element in the cost/revenue merger calculus. The post-merger integration manuals of the consulting fraternity contain standard guidelines for the identification of vulnerable segments whose loss would impair merger economics as well as measures which should be taken proactively to keep them on board. The loss of convenience associated with branch closures, change in brand name, frustration with the inevitable service failures and changes in functionality associated with conversion to a new IT platform, the departure of trusted relationship managers – all lead to attrition which must be contained to achieve financial targets from the merger.

Actually measuring either revenue loss or market share attrition, however, is not a simple task. In the case of several banks in our interview series known to have lost market share during the merger period, it was quite difficult to obtain hard numbers. Even in the case of the well-advertised revenue losses incurred in the First Interstate and Core States conversions in the US, figures quoted in the financial press are both contradictory and disputed by management as being exaggerated.

Managers are understandably shy about confirming the extent of such a negative benchmark for merger performance. In several cases with such interviewees as Handelsbanken and HVB, acknowledged losses were attributed at least in part to deliberate efforts to reduce commitments to low priority sectors. On the other hand, our interview with ABN Amro acknowledged the retail losses suffered as a result of an extended merger period and conversion to a totally new platform.

Only in the case of several Spanish members of the 'Class of 1990' merger wave are hard and relevant numbers available for the loss of market share. Thus BCH lost about 3 per cent in domestic market share between 1990 and 1995, while Argentaria actually gained about 1 per cent share in the deposit market between 1987 and 1995. We discuss below the strategic conclusions drawn by their managers for the second and current merger wave from this early experience in branding.

Combating the inevitable introversion of a bank's client-facing staff during the tumultuous merger process can be a major struggle. Chase

Manhattan's Walter Shipley has propagated throughout his organisation the key phrase:

It's our merger, not the customer's

to redirect his colleagues' attention to the vital business of maintaining and building client relationships.

As John Skerritt of Andersen Consulting confirms:

The first thing in a merger is to work at customer retention. It's obvious that other financial institutions will target your best clients and that there will inevitably be some churn in the client base. Wells Fargo in its First Interstate deal lost sight of that. If it happens, you're always behind the game as you lose revenue faster than you cut costs and end up in a downward spiral.

The consensus of the retail bankers we interviewed is that, in a typical in-market merger, a well-executed merger process would limit the customer – and revenue – loss to about 5–10 per cent of the relevant total. We discuss below the impact of a more significant loss.

In the corporate sector, when two major corporate banks merge in the same market, a certain loss is inevitable as large corporate clients insist on a minimum level of diversification of their banking relationships. Many of the banks reviewed, such as UBS and Deutsche Bank, have incorporated this estimated loss in their forecast of net merger benefits.

In Europe, the issue of brand loyalty adds an extra dimension to the revenue loss equation. In Austria, the UK, Portugal and Spain, for example, banks have consciously retained existing brands – and the costs that go with them – so as to retain the maximum potential revenue base. As the Spanish banks enter their second round of bank mergers in the past decade, they recall the market share loss incurred when they replaced old with new brands in the early 1990s. José Luis del Valle of Banco Santander Central Hispano (BSCH) recalls the earlier merger of Central and Hispano Americano:

We learned a lot about single-brand strategy. People in the branches were primarily worried about the integration. They didn't think about the business – just 'will my branch close?' The network just lost momentum. By maintaining three brands we may initially get fewer savings, but in the first months of the BSCH merger we haven't lost market share. We are now integrating the systems, and if necessary we can always switch later to a new, common brand.

BUILDING A NEW BANK IMPLIES BOTH NEW COSTS AND REVENUES!

One of the painful lessons learned by bank analysts is that merger cost savings are only one element of the overall cost dynamics. A host of added costs – some voluntary, some inevitable – usually accompany the merger process. As we shall discuss in more detail in Chapter 9, the development of modified or new IT systems entails incremental spending which may well exceed the savings from closing down old legacy systems. Anecdotal evidence from our interviews indicates that overruns in IT budgets are frequent – as well as hidden in overall cost figures outside the headline merger savings.

In addition, when the merger is used as an opportunity to transform the new bank, a host of investment costs can accompany the merger. Arguably the most interesting recent case study is that of Swedbank, whose stock was pummelled in 1998 as analysts realised that such costs would dwarf the savings attributed publicly to the 1997 merger with Forenings Sparbanken. Strategic planner Soren Andersson describes the situation:

> In our 1997 merger as well as when Swedbank was created by merger in 1992, we used the merger to transform and restructure the bank as well as cut costs. We offered in 1997 a generous retirement plan to those over 57, enabled all staff who didn't feel comfortable with the new vision to leave after extensive re-training, and invested heavily in new retail systems and staff training. We had a terrible problem explaining this to the market. We've spent billions of kroner to reduce costs. If we want to move into the new banking world, we have to invest in it as well as pay tribute to the old world! And the latter is a question of credibility.

In Spain, BBV's need to build an entirely new IT platform – as well as an extended merger period – depressed its financial results well beyond the merger period. Thus its 1988 merger generated soaring costs which inflated the cost/income ratio above 60 per cent with a return to a more normal 56 per cent only in 1995.

Overshadowing the entire debate over value creation in banking by merger is the extent of transformation needed to create such value on a sustainable basis. In other words, how does management truly make two and two equal five? Economists argue that market values in an open capital market already reflect the potential value of the franchise, so that a buyer/merger partner must have the unique ability to extract additional value to justify paying a premium. At Wells Fargo, Dick Kovacevich's answer is clear: the transformation is a fundamental one.

For bank analysts and managements alike, the Citigroup merger is a bellwether experiment. The product and client breadth they represent, the high regard in which their managements are held, and their steadfast strategic commitment to generate value by enhanced revenue growth – all have focused attention on this role model. As James McDermott, former CEO of investment bank Keefe, Bruyette and Woods, argues, the success of the deal is:

> all in the execution. It can be very effective if they integrate properly; a horror show if they don't.[2]

A corollary of this argument is that cost reduction strategy by serial mergers sooner or later runs out of steam and must be supplemented by one which fuels revenue growth. John Rolander, a vice president at Gemini Consulting, articulates this view:

> In-market mergers have been successful at cost reduction but don't generate long term growth. The solution is complementary mergers, but these have had an absymal track record because of the need to manage different cultures.

A number of issues are raised by these findings and will be analysed in the chapters to follow. First, to what extent are the projected savings actually achieved in practice? Second, does it make sense to project savings when aggregate financial targets are more appropriate and less misleading? Third, are cost-saving mergers adequate to achieve long-term performance targets? How long can banks rely on such saves, as opposed to strategies which promote major revenue gains?

4 Planning the Merger: The First Hundred Days

With this chapter we begin our analysis of the execution process. What steps should be taken, in what sequence, by whom, and over what time frame? The starting point for this process is the overall integration concept. On the basis of our universe, one can broadly segment the alternative concepts into three basic categories:

- *federation*: relatively autonomous operating units continuing to function largely as they did before the merger but with some central control and other common functions
- *best of both*: creating coherent operating units, usually on a line-of-business basis, which maximise cost and revenue synergies as well as creating a single integrated entity able to capitalise on its new structure
- *transforming merger*: creating a truly new entity with a totally different cost structure, revenue profile and/or profit potential from that of the combined predecessor banks

Among our universe, the federal model is typified by banks like ING and Kapital Holding. Most of our universe falls into the 'best of both' category: ABN/Amro, Fleet Boston, BBV, and Bank Austria are cases in point.

The relatively sparse segment of transformed banks might include the new Wells Fargo, MeritaNordbanken, Chase, UniCredito Italiano and Citigroup. Such a transformation is inevitably a long-term effort with a high degree of uncertainty as to the ultimate outcome.

This conceptual decision on strategic goals shapes the key elements of the role of leadership, cultural integration, technology choices, speed of execution, people decisions, and integration processes. Our intent is not to provide a 'how to do it' merger manual but rather to reflect the views of our interviewees on the key lessons of experience. Thus in subsequent chapters we describe in more detail their experience with the central issues of leadership, cultural change, people selection, and choice of major IT systems which preoccupied them.

Having selected which integration concept to adopt, decisions must be made on structure, processes and systems, and extent of physical and

Figure 4.1   Sample task force structure for major bank integration

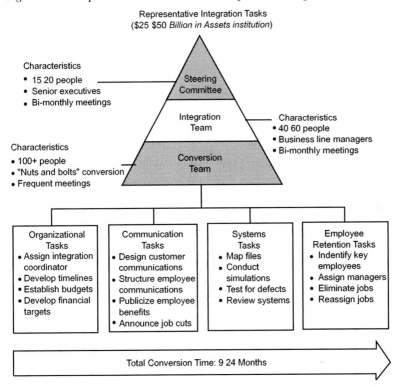

Representative Integration Tasks
($25 $50 *Billion in Assets institution*)

Characteristics
* 15 20 people
* Senior executives
* Bi-monthly meetings

Steering
Committee

Integration
Team

Characteristics
* 40 60 people
* Business line managers
* Bi-monthly meetings

Characteristics
* 100+ people
* "Nuts and bolts" conversion
* Frequent meetings

Conversion
Team

Organizational Tasks	Communication Tasks	Systems Tasks	Employee Retention Tasks
• Assign integration coordinator • Develop timelines • Establish budgets • Develop financial targets	• Design customer communications • Structure employee communications • Publicize employee benefits • Announce job cuts	• Map files • Conduct simulations • Test for defects • Review systems	• Indentify key employees • Assign managers • Eliminate jobs • Reassign jobs

Total Conversion Time: 9 24 Months

Source: Corporate Executive Board Research.

cultural integration. The role of the CEO and the integration leader as well as the overall decision-making process must be defined. Finally, the pace of integration decisions, milestones and time-line, and key decision points must be agreed.

Figures 4.1 and 4.2 illustrate the complexity of the structures, processes and tasks involved. For a bank management undertaking for the first time such a comprehensive and wrenching process, the task is truly a formidable one.

Our interviewees described merger processes involving hundreds of individual projects and thousands of milestones to be met. Among the most comprehensive is Chase's MOM (Merger Overview Model), which for the Chemical/Chase fusion had 56 different integration plans, 3,308 major milestones, 13,000 tasks and 3,820 interdependencies.

Figure 4.2   Sample integration planning structure

- Decision-making body
- Sets overall direction/tone
- Guides effort/resolves conflict
- Review/approves implementation plans
- Monitors overall progress
- Includes senior executives from both institutions, chaired by new CEO

Integration steering committee

Merger office including integration manager

- Design and manage the process
- Resolve policy issues and arbitrate differences
- Ensure high performance aspirations and quality control
- Ensure quick wins and near-term opportunities are captured
- Develop cross-enterprise plans and integrative issues

BU/functional integration
Team A
Team B
Team C
Team D

Cross-functional taskforces

- Develop team charter and end-state blueprints
- Develop detailed execution plan
- Conduct integration with assistance of other teams/CMO
- Includes team leader and staff from both companies

Source: McKinsey & Company.

THE ISSUE OF SPEED

In this chapter we address first the issue of pace of execution, which was cited by almost all the banks interviewed as the dominant lesson of experience. The view of the consultants we met was unanimous: during the first few months – the famous 'hundred days', or what one leading consulting firm calls the stabilisation and preparation phase – key decisions on vision, strategy, financial targets, structure, pace of execution, key people and integration process should be agreed. Speed, communication, discipline and consistency are the words which universally come to their minds. Here are some typical responses:

Nick Viner, a Vice President in the Boston Consulting Group's banking practice, emphasises that:

> You have to move quickly; otherwise the cost savings will be dissipated. You'll lose your best people if you remain in a climate of uncertainty. It's very destabilising, and you need good process to move quickly.

John Skerritt of Andersen Consulting is equally convinced of the virtues of speed and momentum:

Compromise is the enemy of a good merger. It's all about the momentum and drive from top management. You need clarity as to who's in charge. Get the wagon train going! You can't all sit around and discuss where we're going, mixing and matching, and so forth.

And from the academic side, Jane Linder and Dwight Crane, Professors of Finance at The Harvard Business School, agree:

The process is gruelling, but some organizations are better at it than others. Bankers who excel in executing mergers take control of the target institution quickly, consolidate and streamline operations, and take deliberate steps to attract and retain high quality business.[1]

Most of the banks interviewed echo the need for speed – as well as the 'Three Cs' – clarity, communication and consistency. The management of Chase Manhattan, one of the most respected banks for its merger process and results, was able to announce the top 25 members of the new senior management team on the same day it revealed both the ManHan/Chemical and Chemical/Chase mergers. Former CEO Walter Shipley points to the need for crisp decision-making:

It isn't necessary to wait until 100 per cent of the information is assembled and checked – often 70 per cent is enough to move on. Slowness creates uncertainty, and uncertainty – especially in the stressful environment of integrating a merger – can be corrosive and eroding. Uncertainty also breeds conflicts.[2]

Mark Garvin of Chase summarises his own conclusions:

In a merger, implementation precedes optimisation. It's easy to forget that the goal is to get to the finish line. As professionals you are all striving for perfection and want to get it right. The temptation is to try to optimise as you go along. But you don't have time to get it all right because of the pressure to execute the merger. So you go with what you have. Action takes priority over thought, and this means you come back later to tidy things up. Time is truly of the essence.

The same focus on speed in decision-making is articulated across the Atlantic. Matias Inciarte, Vice Chairman of BSCH and one of the four members of its 'G4' executive group, emphasises the importance of timing in announcing the first major bank merger following the introduction of the € in January, 1999:

All our division heads were named on the day of our merger announcement, and we set our objectives for the next few years on the same day. You need clarity from the outset to establish and maintain the momentum.

His colleague José Luis del Valle, who helped direct the merger of two of BSCH's predecessor banks in the early 1990s, agrees:

Our mistake in 1991 in BCH was not to have moved fast enough. It took seven months then to legally conclude our merger. We did it this time over three months.

Andreas Treichl, the CEO of Erste Bank in Austria, emphasises both speed and clarity in their merger with GiroCredit:

The two key lessons were that you need incredibly clear language from the start and you should not look for perfection but rather for speed. We signed the letter of intent in March, 1997, had virtually all the top management named by September, and concluded the transaction in October.

'The first hundred days' is a phrase we heard frequently from both consultants and senior bankers. Within that period, hopefully all key decisions should be made: the type of bank to be created, the strategies needed to achieve that strategic goal, the cultural profile of the new bank, the organisational structure and key people to run it, the issues which are likely to be encountered, and the major operational decisions to be made.

THE TRADE-OFF BETWEEN SPEED AND OTHER VARIABLES

But speed must be tempered by other variables. One such key element, as discussed above, is the type of merger envisaged: federation, best of both or transformation.

Speed – as well as the 'Three Cs' of clarity, communication and consistency – is clearly central to the planning of the second category of mergers which simply bolt the two banks together with a varying degree of attention paid to picking the best dimensions of each. The vast majority of mergers by number fall in this category.

Thus for banks like Fleet, BSCH, Chase, Erste, First Union, UBS, and Deutsche Bank, the challenge is to move as quickly as possible to make these key decisions and join the banks at the operational level. At

Deutsche Bank, Scott Moeller, who co-ordinates the integration teams in London for the key Global Corporates and Institutions Division in its acquisition of Bankers Trust, recalls the lessons from Deutsche Bank's earlier efforts at acquiring an investment banking entity:

> Deutsche's management drew a lot of lessons from the Morgan Grenfell acquisition in 1989. It was long and drawn out. This time Rolf Breuer [the spokesman for the Management Board] has been very explicit: move very fast with aggressive deadlines, which we've met, to create an integrated company. We went through a rigorous process of identifying redundancies and quickly communicated the conclusions to the people involved. They were told of their status in January of 1999 for a merger which actually closed in June of that year.

The decision-making process is totally different for banks taking the federative approach. Hessel Lindenbergh of ING explains that it takes time for people and institutions to get to know each other:

> Particularly in a cross-border merger, where each company has a different culture and business principles, you need to take time for decisions. We made no major changes in BBL for the first year after buying it, and with BHF [recently acquired in 1999] we're just starting to learn about each other. With a federation, you need to take more time – it's a slow and natural process.

Even where speed of decision-making is acknowledged as a necessary attribute, getting to know key executives can be a precondition to such decisions. Bernard Michel of Credit Agricole describes the process of familiarising himself with the key executives at Credit Agricole Indosuez and at the same time debating strategy and structure:

> We didn't name the top people at the beginning. We had to make sure they were the right ones with the right attitude toward the merger. After three months we had a good idea both of their qualifications and attitude, and we could move to integrate the activities within a six-month time frame.

The ABN Amro merger in the early 1990s required an even longer time frame for the key people decisions. Senior Executive Vice President Wilco ten Berg explains:

We started with co-heads of all key functions; eventually one took over the job. Yes, we had too many people at the top, but few were unhappy. It's friendly – the Dutch way of doing it! You can get clarity on day one, but you a make a lot of people unhappy.

The Bayerische Hypo Vereinsbank merger brought together two archrivals in a highly charged political environment. A former senior executive makes a common criticism:

The major lesson was the slow speed of integration. It took six months to announce the members of the Management Board. It took another six for the second tier of management. Compromises were made with constituencies outside the bank which split the management and stalled the decision-making process.

Stefan Ermisch, Senior Vice President of Hypo Vereinsbank, describes the dilemma:

You must make quick decisions – right or wrong. When you bring two cultures together, with lots of people in new jobs, with new bosses and new surroundings, people naturally want to discuss things. You have to have a dialogue, but only up to a point. As for political involvement, we have to recognise that we live in a political world.

A number of our interviewees believe strongly that flexibility is a key ingredient in planning the merger, particularly in a federal structure. Roberto Nicastro of UniCredito points out that:

You have to be flexible, depending on the bank involved. If you have a high performing bank (like Rolo Banca) you don't want much interference. In other cases, you have to move very fast to make big changes.

Fortis and Den Danske Bank also agree on the need for flexibility. Putting out fires or responding to a deteriorating economic environment require urgent action. Henjo Hielkema of Fortis describes the acquisition of control of ASLK/CGER, a government-owned savings bank managed by political appointees:

After extended negotiations with the Belgian government, as soon as we had 50 per cent control we had to move fast to achieve dramatic consequences, particularly in the loan book. We moved in a new management team on day one and ruthlessly removed the old one. It was difficult at the time, but it gave a signal that the politicians had ceased to have influence in the bank.

Leonhardt Pihl, head of strategy for Den Danske Bank, contrasts the more recent acquisition of the Danica insurance group with the 1990 three-way merger which created the bank in a difficult economic environment.

In 1990 we had to get things done very fast. The credit market was deteriorating quickly and we had to establish a new structure. Rather than have co-heads [as did rival Unibank] we went right to the final structure. It was not a very democratic process and there were a lot of dissatisfied people.

Perhaps the most interesting merger typology is the creation of a totally new bank. Decisions on strategy, structure and processes understandably may take more time than in a 'bolt together' merger, yet all agree that decisions should be made in a disciplined fashion. One of the most interesting examples of such an approach is that of the new Wells Fargo. Under the leadership of Dick Kovacevich from the former Norwest, one of the most highly regarded CEOs in US banking, Wells is truly a different bank from its predecessors: As Kovacevich explains:

I would argue that, if the new company is exactly like the old one with a high price paid as well, how can you possibly create value – like two plus two equals five? The only way is to merge with someone who has different values. Either two plus two equals three or it equals five. You need to take the best of both possible worlds. So when we sat down with the management of the old Wells we said that, to do a deal, we had to reach agreement in advance on strategy, structure, philosophy, IT and values – what we all believed in. We showed them our value statement and they agreed it was consistent with theirs. Before you sign the papers you have to eliminate any ambiguity.

Another advocate of thinking through the merger in advance of any commitment is John McCoy, former CEO of Bank One and major influence in creating the merger of equals with First Chicago NBD. He describes a similar conversation with his counterpart at First Chicago, who wanted to follow up earlier preliminary discussions by debating financial terms, headquarters location and other issues:

> I suggested we first sit down and review how we each run our businesses. We each had different structures, but Vern Istock agreed that ours made sense. Then we sat down and went through all the senior people. In a day we were able to pick heads of 18 of the top 20 jobs. So in two days we had decided how and who to run the company. Then we started to talk about price and headquarters.

The strongest objection to speed, of course, is making serious strategic errors. Within our universe of recent mergers, these errors are legion. We discuss in the next chapter the pitfalls of the due diligence process, but suffice it to say here that a host of major asset quality and other problems were not identified at the due diligence stage in our merger universe.

On the people side, there has been a host of key executive appointments which had to be jettisoned shortly after the merger announcement and which might have been averted by a more deliberate decision-making pace. Thus the former CEOs of the old UBS, Bank of America, Bayerische Hypo Bank, and Bankers Trust all left under a cloud soon into the merger process. In the words of Rolf Breuer, head of Deutsche Bank, referring to former CEO Frank Newman of Bankers Trust who had been slated for a post on the group's *Vorstand* but was found to be unpopular even among the former Bankers Trust management:

> You have to get much closer before they tell you about such things.[3]

Excessive speed was directly responsible for the two recent well-advertised examples of poor merger execution by experienced merger practitioners in the US. The purchase of First Interstate by the old Wells Fargo and the acquisition of Core States by First Union have become business school case studies in how not to execute a big bank merger. Having paid an aggressive price for an attractive regional franchise, each buyer set an equally ambitious merger plan in terms of cost saves and timetable. The result was customer and staff disaffection and revenue loss which destroyed the merger's economics. Austin Adams, Executive Vice President of First Union, reflects on the dilemma:

> The issue is the ability of an acquired institution to assimilate change. We paid five times book value and aimed at a 40 per cent expense

reduction with a 12-month conversion period. At the same time we were totally revamping our Future Bank retail platform. In retrospect, while much of the transition went well, it was asking too much to expect thousands of people, often new in their jobs, as well as customers, to significantly change their behaviour in the time frame we set.

Another issue which constrains management's ability to move expeditiously is commitments to external constituencies. Particularly in Europe, political, regulatory and administrative barriers pose serious challenges to the merger process. In the Kapital Holding merger, BG Bank has been unable to merger operationally with its mortgage provider Realkredit because of legal constraints. The same has been true of Den norske Bank's purchase of the Vital insurance company, while Credit Suisse's acquisition of Winterthur was predicated on the insurer's retaining its corporate identity. To achieve its merger with Creditanstalt, Bank Austria had to commit to the Austrian government that Creditanstalt should retain its separate identity for five years.

Some of these constraints are self-imposed in the form of commitments to management or sellers to make the merger possible, while others are inherent in the local political and legal environment. In Germany, the Bayerische Hypo Vereinsbank and LBBW mergers were strongly influenced by the agendas of the key political players.

Other constraints are imposed by the need to obtain the approval of the unions and work councils which play a central role in most of the European countries. Several of our interviewees in France, the Netherlands, Austria and Belgium described in vivid detail the efforts which had to be made to convince employee representatives to agree steps necessary to achieve the merger's strategic objectives. One of our Belgian friends notes with satisfaction that union representatives present at a mass meeting of his merged bank being addressed by the CEO kept their whistles – usually employed to drown out the voice of the speaker – in their pockets in the knowledge that their members broadly supported the transaction.

In Japan, such commitments have shaped an extended merger process. Several of the planned three fusions of major banks are characterised as consolidations, not mergers, with actual functional integration not scheduled to take place for two years. The extended time period is attributed to the need for regulatory and other approvals, which at a minimum extends the period of uncertainty and may reinforce resistance to change. In some cases it is not clear whether true integration or a federal structure is the ultimate goal.

FRIENDLY VS. UNFRIENDLY MERGERS

Another key issue raised by our interviews is whether the merger is a friendly or unfriendly one. The widely held view is that this characteristic shapes both the ability to reach agreement on a deal as well as its implementation. Thus a wide range of senior bankers at Chase, ABN Amro, Bank One, ING, Lloyds TSB, Credit Agricole, Merita Nordbanken and Wells Fargo emphasised that they would only contemplate such transactions where management presumably welcomes the merger.

Thus both Walter Shipley of Chase and John McCoy of Bank One point to their ability to attract merger partners who might not otherwise be interested in a deal – as well as the obviously better internal climate for executing it. By the same token, Tom Grondahl of Den norske Bank, which acquired the Vital insurance company by successfully bidding against a foreign partner welcomed by Vital management, acknowledges that:

> We were a 'black knight' [as opposed to a white one] for Vital, and there was resistance in the beginning to the merger.

In markets like Spain and the Netherlands, there would appear to be a cultural bias toward transactions which are perceived as friendly. Thus Wilco ten Berg of ABN Amro and Matias Inciarte of BSCH note that such an environment is essential for successful execution in their national cultures.

On closer examination, however, the issue is more complex. First, many mergers are consummated with a considerable degree of reluctance on the part of one of the banks whose management recognises that market forces oblige them to do a deal and that their choice may be limited to which partner they can select. The apocryphal telephone call made by an institutional investor, Michael Price, to the CEO of the old Chase Manhattan suggesting a merger with the stronger Chemical Bank, is one indication of the pressure which can be applied by determined institutional investors. Another is the 'bear hug' approach of a predator who can force apparent agreement by the threat of making a take-out market bid. Whether the extra price paid to convert an 'unfriendly' deal into a 'friendly' one will actually facilitate the merger process is an open question.

Secondly, some mergers start as presumably friendly, agreed deals but become acrimonious because of an unexpected negative event and/

or the departure of a key executive whose presence was essential to knitting together the two cultures. We discuss in Chapter 8 in more detail the impact on mergers such as those of Hypo Vereinsbank, BBV, original Bank Austria and UBS mergers of such a 'bump on the road' which creates acrimony in an already strained environment.

Conversely, a supposedly unfriendly merger stemming from a contested take-over bid or sale over the head of management by a controlling stockholder can become essentially a friendly one. For example, the Bank Austria/Creditanstalt merger began as a take-over vigorously resisted by the CEO and many executives of Creditanstalt concerned about their purchase by their traditional rival. The opponents soon left the merged bank, but, as Danilo Melamed of Bank Austria acknowledges:

Creditanstalt was taken by surprise by our successful offer. But the individual implementation decisions were openly negotiated in an environment of meritocracy, and what has emerged is a friendly merger – some would even say a partial take-over by Creditanstalt!

His colleague from the Creditanstalt side, Alois Steinbichler of Bank Austria Creditanstalt International, confirms the transformation:

While it may have appeared unfriendly at the beginning, a more pragmatic view was soon established. Those who stayed behind tend to take a professional, rather than emotive position. We see it as a management challenge.

The same pragmatism has been reflected in the continued presence in the combined top management of a number of other banks in our universe of executives from the target bank. Thus senior managers from Générale Bank, Banco Portugues do Atlantico and Giro Credit all now appear on the combined management boards of banks who succeeded with unfriendly bids or took over a bank by a deal with its stockholders.

Outside our universe, our sources note the widespread popping of champagne corks in Banque Paribas dealing rooms when the presumably friendly Société Générale bid was defeated by the 'unfriendly' Banque Nationale de Paris offer in 1999. Not only investment bankers but many others take a pragmatic view of their career prospects whatever their stockholders or superiors might conclude!

We discuss in Chapter 7 in more detail the techniques used to create a more positive environment after an often bitter initial conflict.

THE VALUE OF EXPERIENCE

The good news is that experience in executing successive mergers clearly facilitates the task for future transactions. There is no doubt in the minds of our interviewees that serial merger banks are more successful than those embarking on their first major deal. One of the points made by the consultants we interviewed is that managing a merger historically has occupied a very small portion of a typical bank CEO's career. As Nick Viner of BCG puts it:

> For most management of a bank, leading a merger is a completely new experience – it's never happened before.

His view is echoed by Norman Bernard of First Consulting:

> Managing a big merger is a small window in a CEO's career; they have not previously suffered the pain when things go wrong. Nowadays a corporate financier sells the idea, the CFO agrees the terms, and the CEO is made to feel terribly important: then suddenly the deal is done and they're all alone!'

The merger wave in the US and Europe may be turning this argument on its head. Not only serial acquirers like the old Nationsbank, Bank One and Fleet Boston have developed finely honed machines to absorb other banks, but also competitors like Chase have learned from experience. In Europe, the 'Class of 1990' has been followed by the second wave of current mergers to create national champions and, eventually, cross-border mergers. As Bank One's John McCoy puts it:

> It's like any sporting event – you have to practice to become a quarterback in the National Football League.

In the words of Tom Grondahl of Den norske Bank as it enters its second major merger of the decade with Postbanken, when confronted with a merger issue:

> We can just take out the old material, dust it off, and know exactly how we did it in the past.

The role of outside consultants appears to have changed as well. For their first major merger, most of the European banks we met used teams of up to 50 and more professionals from leading consulting firms to manage the extraordinarily complex execution process. For their second deal, they seem to be relying generally on this experience and using consultants for more specialist tasks such as deciding on future IT platforms and assisting in the selection of management personnel from the merging entities.

The end product of the merger preparation process can be a time frame which varies widely – for both predictable and unforeseen reasons. Thus Table 4.1 profiles the consolidation of eight members of the 'class of 1990': European banks which fused in anticipation of the introduction of the single European market in 1992. The critical period projected to create a single banking system varied from a lean six months in the case of DnB in Norway to 45 in the case of ABN Amro. The latter decided to build a new system based on those of its component banks, while DnB benefited from the common systems used among Norwegian stockholder-owned banks.

Another view of the actual variations in the critical time line of a merger is demonstrated in Figure 4.3, which contrasts three recent major European mergers.

Merger C thus suffered from a relatively slow start in selecting management, accentuated by a long preparatory effort and a 'best of breed' philosophy.

Table 4.1 The 'class of 1990': mergers in anticipation of EU '92

Merged Institution	Date of merger announcement	Combined share of domestic retail banking	Months to create single banking system	Planned staff reduction(%)
ABN/Amro (Netherlands)	3/90	30%E	45	9 (over 5 years)
BBV (Spain)	1/88	20E	9	15 (over 5 years)
Bank Austria (Austria)	4/91	12	35	11 (over 4 years)
NMB/Postbank (Netherlands)	10/89	23	NR	NR
DNB (Norway)	10/89	15	6	13–14 (in 2 years)
Unibank (Denmark)	12/89	30	30–36	10 (in 3 years)
Den Danske (Denmark)	11/89	25	24	10 (in 2–3 years)
Ambroveneto (Italy)	2/89	2.3	NA	9 (over 5 years)

Source: DIBC research.
NR = Not relevant; NA = Not available.

Figure 4.3 Differential performance in pace of integration use

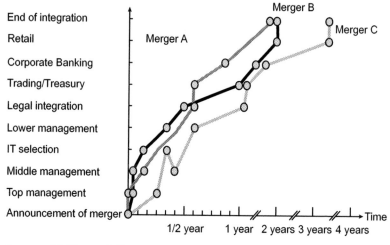

Source: McKinsey & Company.

A number of issues are thrown up by this analysis. One is whether the exceptions to the 'hundred day' rule are sustainable ones. Can, for example, an ING or Citigroup afford to take a relaxed view on some of these key decisions? What decisions must be made early in the game, and which deferred to a later period?

Secondly, how much of a barrier to successful integration is a so-called unfriendly merger? Can effective leadership and strong process overcome initial resistance?

We shall address these issues in subsequent chapters.

5 The Due Diligence Process: Safety Net or Nuisance?

An integral part of the merger process is the preliminary screening for asset quality and other problems once a merger has been agreed in principle. Such a vetting would seem to be crucial in a business like banking with its central focus on risk. And another bank familiar with these risks, especially one with such a profound interest in the outcome, would appear to be a most effective agent to uncover problems and evaluate the findings. Finally, the example of several asset quality bombs which in the past have exploded shortly after a bank merger closing would seem to constitute a red flag for those undertaking new transactions.

The findings from our interview series do not, to say the least, support this optimistic view.

Understandably, unfriendly bids without the benefit of any form of access to a target's books constitute an inevitable risk which hopefully is incorporated in the terms of the bid. One of the few such contested bids reviewed, the purchase of BPA by BCP in Portugal, was made without the benefit of anything more than the rudimentary historical data available on a publicly quoted company in Portugal. As BCP's Pedro Libano Monteiro explains:

> The figures were not as clear as we had thought. There were some real estate and other non-bank investments, and we had to take some unexpected provisions. There was some extra effort but it was not a disaster.

What is much more surprising, however, is the virtually unanimous view of our universe that conducting due diligence, even between willing partners essentially opening up their books to each other, does not constitute a very reliable safety net. The litany of negative comment is long and decisive: here are some sample comments from our interviews on the value of due diligence:

- Hessel Lindenbergh of ING: 'We knew BBL and BHF [their two European acquisitions] well, but in general due diligence is only as good as a doctor's guarantee after a physical exam – only good until you leave his office!'

- Roberto Nicastro of UniCredito: 'Obviously you have to do it, but frankly it just leads to painful discussions. You never find a big black hole. You find problems, but rarely a deal breaker.'
- Dick Kovacevich of Wells Fargo: 'In a big merger of equals, it's impossible to do an exhaustive due diligence because of the size and need for confidentiality. So for such deals we carry out a so-called "executive review" to identify the major problem areas – i.e. with loss potential of over $1 billion, the big elephants – and absorb smaller losses in the purchase price.'
- Scott Moeller of Deutsche Bank: 'For practical purposes you do due diligence because you need to find if there are major problems. But you can never find everything in a few weeks of due diligence even with the best experts; only when you've put the organisations together can you find if there is any hidden "nuclear waste".'

One of the most telling indictments of the value of due diligence comes from a senior banker with one of the major US serial acquirers:

> In the early 1980s we were babes in the woods in terms of due diligence. In the early 1990s with the failed S & Ls [savings banks] we got good data on the failed banks and developed the right disciplines. So under the modern agenda we send in teams and run models and feel pretty good about the risks. But in the panic psychology of the late 1990s it's really 'close your eyes' once again – the same story as in the 1980s except that you're talking much bigger numbers!

The due diligence problem is particularly agonising for banks which have suffered grievously from losses which arguably might have been identified by a thorough due diligence conducted on a willing partner.

A classic case study of an undetected loss threatening the viability of a merger is that of Hypo Vereinsbank. The DM 3.5 billion write-off in the former Hypo loan book announced shortly after the closing of the 1997 merger resulted two years later in the resignation of all of the Hypo members of the combined management board as well as a massive on-going distraction of management time from the merger process. How could this have happened, particularly when Hypo was known to have been an aggressive lender in the troubled East German real estate market? As Stefan Ermisch of Hypo Vereinsbank explains,

> A big merger of equals has to be based on trust – it's like a marriage. You don't ask all the nasty questions. Our deal was based on the independent auditor's report, and management and the supervisory board trusted them.

A more cynical view is expressed by a journalist who noted the extensive number of external audits and the departure in 1999 of board members from Hypo Bank who had nothing to do with its real estate portfolio:

> It is more about politics and the credibility of bank management than numbers. One section of the Bavarian mafia [Schmidt of Vereinsbank] took on another [Martini of Hypo] and played a numbers game to beat him![1]

Another loss which crystallised after due diligence and merger completion was the former UBS' exposure to Long Term Capital Management (LTCM) and its global equity derivative book at the time of the SBC/UBS merger. The subsequent write-down threw results for the first post-merger year off track as well as damaged the credibility of the risk management skills of the former SBC management. UBS' CEO Marcel Ospel acknowledges that:

> SBC didn't have a clue [about the hidden exposure], and UBS didn't either. We weren't hiding anything and SBC could not have exercised more due diligence before the deal. Nonetheless, it's a wake-up call for the whole industry.

While credit and market risk losses are usually the most visible and painful for a bank, there are others as well which in theory should be identified by the thorough due diligence which banks usually conduct on their own clients. One such example of operational risk was that of Handelsbanken when it took over the specialist mortgage lender Stadshypotek. In its focus on credit and market risk, the highly regarded Handelsbanken team did not spend enough time on systems compatibility when planning for cross-selling and product integration. As Lars Gronstedt, Executive Vice President of Handelsbanken explains:

> Proportionally, we spent too much time on due diligence where, in retrospect, everything was pretty much as we thought it was. No one looked at the company's IT and the mismatch between the two systems. There was a cultural glitch because we didn't speak the same language.

Why should due diligence be of such marginal value even between friendly partners? Quite simply because they are so friendly. Just as our sources universally put little faith in the practice, they agree on the reluctance of merger partners to threaten an otherwise positive and blooming relationship. Rudi Bogni of UBS' management board, who managed the due diligence for its acquisition of SG Warburg and is familiar with the due diligence with the old UBS, puts it as follows:

> It's a question of what is feasible. If you're a buyer of a bank and can walk away from the deal, you can get quite far in your due diligence. But if it's a merger – especially of equals – you have to be gentle. People get upset – or walk! You tiptoe around, do your best, and focus on the major areas like credit risk, but there are clear limits on what you can establish.

Management consultant John Rolander puts it in more graphic language:

> In a merger you're on two different emotional tracks. On the one hand, you're an engaged couple building positive empathy. But you're also trying to check to see if your partner has AIDS. It's hard to run on both tracks. And you don't want to draw the due diligence process out because you want to save time. One of our clients had to fire his head of due diligence because of what was found after the process.

Even knowing your partner well does not guarantee success in identifying problems. Erste Bank's Andreas Treichl and his colleagues had sat on the Board of Directors of GiroCredit, in which their bank had had a substantial equity interest for decades before the acquisition in 1997. Yet as he acknowledges:

> There were significant surprises in the portfolio as well as the quality of some of the people. It was worse than we had thought.

As is clear from the comment above from our US banking friend, merger mania and the desire to conclude a deal militate against the thorough, objective due diligence which would seem to be necessary to avert the nasty surprises which have dogged many of the banks interviewed. As one of our sources commented:

> If the top people want to do the deal, it will happen (regardless of the due diligence process).

Placed in a longer-term framework, the weakness of the due diligence process is an indication of the broader unknowns faced by all merger parties. Several senior bankers volunteered the comment that several years are necessary to evaluate one's partner. We have already noted the view of bankers like Hessel Lindenbergh, who wants to spend a year or so together in a federation to become familiar with each other before taking any major strategic decision. Bankers like Andreas Treichl and Bill Crozier, formerly CEO of BayBanks, one of the most respected US regional banks before becoming part of the current Fleet Boston, agree that a merger resembles a marriage where the partners do not truly understand each other until they have been together for several years. The same parallel with marriage is echoed by Mark Garvin of Chase, who has traversed two mergers of former competitors:

You *think* you know your competitors until you merge with them!

One of the most poignant case studies of due diligence is that of Bank of America. Dave Coulter, the former CEO of the old Bank of America, was quoted in a November, 1998 article fretting about the hidden risks in target portfolios:

I've never seen a positive due diligence surprise.[2]

By the time the article was published, Coulter had resigned under pressure following the revelation of $1.2 billion in unexpected losses from his own bank's portfolios.

The major issue raised by these findings is thus how to reconcile, on the one hand, the desire to win the hand of a partner and to move swiftly though the implementation process, and on the other to carry out an objective and thorough evaluation process with the information available. We address this dilemma in the subsequent chapters.

6 Leadership: The Essential Ingredient

Merging two (or more!) large and complex institutions generates conflict on a grand scale. The textbook solution to this conflict is leadership of an equally high standard. Not surprisingly, we found an almost unanimous agreement that extraordinary leadership is central to resolving the myriad conflicts in the merger process and channelling these energies into building a new banking institution.[1]

The consultants in particular highlight the role of leadership in the merger process. Thus John Skerritt of Andersen Consulting is unequivocal:

> Mergers are all about drive from top management and maintaining momentum. The best mergers are those with a powerful CEO who drives it through. There is no lack of clarity as to who's in charge.

Nick Viner of BCG points to what happens in the absence of such strong leadership:

> Not taking decisions early in the process means things don't happen. Uncertainty is perpetuated and other people's agendas come to dominate.

These views are echoed by the bank executives themselves, who repeat the mantra of consistency, communication and clarity. Bank One's John McCoy believes that:

> There has to be one CEO and everyone has to understand that. We have lots of discussion of merger issues and we want to build consensus, and in the event of a disagreement we talk it out. But in the event of a tie I get the deciding vote. We ask each head of a function how he's going to run his business, and we establish a budget and a road map. Then I have to put out the brush fires.

Erste Bank's Treichl focuses on the challenges of communication and consistency:

> From the start you need to communicate clearly and not change direction. We spend a lot of time propagating the new culture. We do

road shows within the bank; in the first 12 months after the merger, I saw all 9,000 employees twice. A year later, we all got together in the same room. It cost a lot of time and money – and perhaps it wasn't enough!

From our interviews we collected a number of anecdotes on the leadership styles of the various CEOs. One of the most interesting is that of Hans Dalborg, the Swedish Chief Executive of MeritaNordbanken. As the head of the first major European cross border merger, his task of bringing different cultures together has been particularly challenging. His Finnish colleague Ari Laakso points with awe to his linguistic skills:

Dalborg understands the meaning of communication. He is one of the few foreigners who have taken the trouble to learn Finnish [not one of the easiest languages!] so he can read a statement in a press conference in Finnish and communicate with the rest of us. The Finns see that he's trying to be the boss of us too.

Our poll of successful merger leaders places Walt Shipley of Chase at the top of the league. For Shipley, trust and commitment to a 'win–win' future are key elements of his leadership philosophy:

You need to create an environment where both sides feel they are winning. With my counterparts from ManHan and Chase, we all had to suppress the need to feed our egos. At the top we created a visible partnership and articulated the model to the rest of the bank. You have to trust each other to be honest about people. We had to move quickly and didn't have the luxury of getting to know the other bank's people. If we looked at the personnel files and realised we both had good people for a job and if John McGillicuddy [of ManHan] still strongly backed his guy, I tended to support him. When you feel part of a meritocracy, it works better.

A number of banks in our universe have adopted a formula whereby the CEO – usually from the dominant bank – chooses one or more key subordinates from the partner to share an 'office of the chairman' top management group. The single CEO is clearly in charge, but there is enough shared responsibility involving executives from the other bank to ensure representation from both predecessor institutions. Thus Bank One, Chase, Wells Fargo in the US as well as BSCH, Bank Austria,

Erste Bank and ING in Europe incorporate senior representation from their partner institution in the top executive team. The decision in 1999 to remove all former Hypo Bank executives from HVB's *Vorstand*, in contrast, clearly makes the leadership task more difficult.

Leadership in a federal structure poses special challenges. Alessandro Profumo, the CEO and architect of the UniCredito group, must deal with CEOs of acquired banks who have been used to running their own show as well as their Boards of Directors who have resisted the loss of their influence. As his colleague Roberto Nicastro puts it:

> Dealing with other CEOs in a federal structure is tougher. But his charisma and drive enable him to break through resistance.

Dick Kovacevich at Wells Fargo is widely viewed as one of the most admired leaders in US banking today. He emphasises the need for long-term change, a patient approach to managing change, and the twin guidelines of communication and consistency:

> In implementing a merger, process is more important than the result. Everyone assumes he has the answer. There are two ways to do it: either no discussion to achieve speed and efficiency, or taking the time to educate people. It's like the tortoise and the hare: it seems slower but it isn't. Decisions are made by the people themselves; 'it's our decision'! These things take a long time to do right. There are three rules of leadership: communication, communication and communication. If there's another, its consistency, consistency and consistency. People are always saying 'do they really mean it?'

THE ISSUE OF COLLECTIVE LEADERSHIP

Opinions differ on the issue of collective leadership in its various forms. In Europe and Japan, consensus management is more the norm than the exception it is in the US. In particular, the concept of the *Vorstand*, or management board with collective responsibility, dominates the scene in countries like the Netherlands and Germany. Here the Chairman of the Management Board is more a first among equals, a speaker for the board, than a decision-maker as is the CEO in the US.

Both Deutsche Bank as well as ING and ABN Amro in the Netherlands thus remain committed to the principle of collective responsibility and leadership. As ING's Hessel Lindenbergh explains,

There's still a big difference between the Anglo-Saxon and non-Anglo-Saxon approaches. In Europe, we're more used to debating and exchanging views. The role of the Chief Executive is changing, particularly in dealing with the outside world such as the investment community. But collegiate responsibility remains, and we still seek consensus internally. There's open debate and a lot of respect for individual personalities.

In the fast-paced world of investment banking, however, many question the ability of such decision-makers to compete successfully with their US rivals who dominate the sector and are headed by Anglo-Saxon-type CEOs. A senior executive of one of the major German banks agrees:

> German institutions produce very poor leadership. It's truly a consensual culture. They can't seem to get the concept of leadership into the culture. So in our bank the decision-making is pushed down the organisation to the people who are actually making the money.

A variant of the *Vorstand* form of collective leadership is the collegiate model of several banks which have grown rapidly by merger. Thus Dexia and Fortis each have a quartet of four senior executives, generally taken from the founding organisations, who share the decision-making task. Henjo Hilkema, one of the four top executives of Fortis, affirms that this model works well:

> Joint leadership is a strength for us. We can provide the right leader to suit the occasion. The four people at the top sign off responsibility to one executive and track his performance. There's a built-in discipline, and it's hard to do it any other way. The top four people are very complementary. But in a cross border merger like ours, it's easy to blame nationality as a scapegoat. We spend a lot of time coming to grips with these differences.

What is clear is that the leader must establish an atmosphere of trust with his senior colleagues. If that bond is broken by a major policy disagreement, the departure of a close colleague, or other traumatic event, the repercussions down the organisational chain become magnified. The ubiquitous 'we and they' syndrome of a merger environment is exacerbated, making the task of the leadership even more difficult. Thus the departure early in the merger process of leaders such as UBS'

Chairman Matias Cabiallavetta, Bank of America's Coulter and Hypo Bank's Eberhard Martini can also be painful for his former colleagues who remain. Wilco ten Berg of ABN Amro puts it well:

> If the top people hate each other, the subordinates respond accordingly. In our merger, we started with co-chief executives, one from ABN and one from Amro. They worked as equals. If there was a conflict, they found a solution by working as equals.

Multiple leadership is often a temporary solution for the early months of a merger period. Thus the co-department heads of ABN Amro eventually were reduced to a single individual, and the tripartite leadership of Unibank departments disappeared with the arrival of a new CEO. The Bank of Spain, when it intervened to settle BBV's leadership problem, insisted on a single CEO. The process may be a gentle one or a gladiatorial context with the stronger personality driving out the other.

Another variant of multiple leadership is the naming of one former CEO to the post of current chief executive to be succeeded after several years by his counterpart, who in the meantime retains a senior executive position. A typical case in point is that of Fleet Boston, where Bank Boston's Chad Gifford is scheduled to succeed Fleet's Terry Murray on his retirement two years after the merger. Landesbank Baden-Wuerttemberg in Stuttgart has taken this formula one step further in a three-way merger by designating a new chairman from each of the three banks for successive two-year periods in office. Perhaps predictably, this has resulted in the departure of the head of the most profitable entity, Landesgirokasse, who drew the short straw as the last of the three chairmen. As an insider in one of the banks comments:

> So the best [CEO] goes last, and they lost the best talent. The joke went around to the effect that, if you get Maradona [the soccer star] on your team, you can't expect him to sit on the bench for four years.

The challenge of such a succession of former CEOs is to maintain clarity and to speak with one voice, particularly in a difficult merger environment. Such a case existed with the formative Bank Austria merger, when the CEO of Z Bank, Rene Haiden, became chief executive to be followed by Gerhard Randa of the old Laenderbank. As one of his Bank Austria colleagues comments:

We had two different people speaking for Bank Austria. You could pick the view you wanted. There was lots of stress. But amazingly it worked!

Whether a single CEO or a collegium provides leadership, the proof of the pudding is in the result. Luis Bastida, Chief Financial Officer of Banco Bilbao Vizcaya and a veteran of BBV's exhausting leadership struggle in the late 1980s, puts his finger on the problem:

> The chief lesson from BBV's experience is not to have divided leadership at the top (with both CEOs from the predecessor banks acting as co-CEOs). Having co-heads works if they get along well and move the bank in the same direction.

The compromises which drive the choice of the multiple leadership model so often generate other compromises in merger execution. The result may be an extended merger period, a compromise on the choice of IT systems or key executive slots, or the decision not to implement demanding staff cuts. On the other hand, as advocates such as Hessel Lindenberg and Wilco ten Berg maintain in extolling 'the Dutch model', it may ensure a vital friendly atmosphere during the difficult early merger years.

BBV is only one of several banks whose merger has been jeopardised by a falling-out between its architects. The departure in 1999 of the HypoBank members of the Hypo Vereinsbank Management Board following the confirmation of the massive real estate losses in Hypo-Bank's portfolio is a serious blow. The UBS merger suffered indirectly as former UBS executives were tarred by the brush of losses in its derivatives book. A similar case was the discovery of heavy losses shortly after the original Bank Austria merger when write-offs in the portfolio inherited from the predecessor bank Laenderbank led to the discrediting and departure of many Laenderbank senior executives. In the strained atmosphere of the merger process, the 'we and they' conflict is easily exacerbated by blaming the 'they' for serious errors.

As in so many other dimensions, the leadership of the Citigroup merger is ploughing new ground. In the diverse universe of bank mergers, it is difficult to find another which is so totally dependent on the personalities and personal agendas of John Reed of Citicorp and Sandy Weill of Travelers who personally shaped and drove the merger. As Jack Morris of Citicorp describes the concept,

They have totally different management styles: Sandy epitomises leadership and intuition on the highest plane, while John is cerebral and concerned with strategy and process. Yet they have a lot of respect for each other and have been through the mill together. The concept from the start is that they will be co-CEOs in every respect. They knew they would have to adapt to each other, and there's been no evidence of friction – no stamping of the foot and leaving the room!

The concept of co-CEOs has been applied liberally at other levels of the organisation as well. In July 1999, well over a year after the merger closed, it was announced in an internal memorandum that Messrs Weill and Reed would no longer run all operations of the group jointly but would divide up certain responsibilities. Weill will run the financial and business operations with Reed focusing on technology, the Internet, human resources and legal issues. Thus ended a period dubbed the 'Noah's Ark approach' by an analyst.

An exceptional leader can convert a supposedly unfriendly merger into one where the 'we and they' mentality is subsumed into real collaboration. Gerhard Randa of Bank Austria and Jorge Jardim Gonçalves of BCP are among those highly regarded by their colleagues from both sides of the merger divide for having created such a meritocracy. Walter Shipley also recalls having to defend himself with his own colleagues against the acquisition of having favoured those from the 'other bank' against his own people who 'wanted to do it "our" way'.

Thorleif Krarup of Unibank is an example of a CEO brought into a bank suffering not only from divisive internal conflict between the merger partners but also severe asset quality problems which threatened its viability. As one friend in Unibank told us:

The logic behind the merger was right, but it was not a happy merger. Market conditions worsened and the cultures of the merging partners were very different. But then [in 1992] Thorleif arrived. He wasn't part of the history. He told us 'I'm from Unibank, not one of the old banks, and we'll create a Unibank culture'.

Krarup describes how he approached the challenge:

Things were more serious than I had realised. First, I told them that I was not bringing in 'my team'. We were going to identify the right people in the bank to run it and get rid of the wrong ones. Second, during the crisis period I said we were going to consolidate decision-making, but that when we emerged from the crisis we would share the success. Thus I would take responsibility when things were not going well. And lastly, I had to show my personality wholeheartedly. I told them I would work like hell to make it a success.

While strong and effective leadership is particularly essential during the tender early months of the merger process, the need continues for years. As we discuss in later chapters, when 'post-merger depression' almost inevitably sets in a year or so after the merger date, the leader must be there to exhort his depressed colleagues. A friend in one of the Austrian banks explains:

We could use even more leadership now [a year after the merger] to demonstrate commitment and excitement and clarify some situations. You need repetition and consistency as ambiguities creep in and new developments occur. We need the 'warm spring rain' of leadership presence to bind it all together.

A disturbing – though probably inevitable – theme in several of our conversations was the phrase 'letting ego get in the way' in referring to a specific CEO. Not only Walter Shipley, but many others noted that successful implementation may require subordination of a leader's testosterone to the need to ensure inclusive and viable execution.

Finally, leadership has become a dangerous sport in an industry which used to be known for guaranteed security. Within our universe, several CEOs have been jettisoned by their respective boards of directors for disagreements on strategy or performance. Thus during the year 1999 alone, the COO of First Union Corporation, John Georgius, felt compelled to resign over problems such as the Core States integration. Forenings Sparbanken's CEO Reinhard Geijer also left over a disagreement over performance, while his board ejected Kapital Holding's CEO Henrik Thufasen. And in December 1999, John McCoy resigned as CEO of Bank One.

Two issues emerge from this analysis. First, given the importance of leadership skills and the proliferation of merger activity, one can legitimately pose the question of how many leaders in the banking industry are capable of demonstrating the unique skills needed to bind together the merging banks. When we asked subordinates about the leadership capabilities of their CEO, the answer did not always match the profile of vision, energy and empathy which most research has indicated to be necessary in a stressful situation.

Second, can multiple leadership survive in a fast-paced banking sector such as investment banking? There is much evidence that a single CEO is essential in a business where major commitments must be made in a time frame which does not allow for consensus to build.

Once again, we shall address these issues in our concluding chapter.

7 Selecting and Motivating People

The ability to select and retain the desired key professionals is one of the central challenges of the merger process. The difficulty of blending speed with fairness and meritocracy in the selection process, the frustrations of top executives facing uncertainty and jockeying for positions in the merger, and the need to satisfy multiple constituencies in job selection all militate against a successful outcome.

THE SELECTION PROCESS

The merger manuals of the major consulting firms understandably argue for identification at the earliest stage of the executives to be retained and an expeditious shortening of the inevitable period of uncertainty over job responsibilities. Most consultants maintain that key jobs should be filled over a maximum period of three–four months – the 'hundred days' cited in an earlier chapter. And the phrases 'meritocracy' and 'transparency' are repeated frequently in their recommendations. A host of formal selection processes exist: the use of an independent consultant, requesting all candidates to apply for jobs, and top-down selection by heads of business units.

In practice, we found a wide variety of approaches to executive selection. At one extreme is the 'our team takes over' typical of many US banks who have developed human and systemic resources to absorb all but the largest acquisitions. At the other is the pure meritocracy advocated by consultants whereby top jobs are filled by a transparent and objective process. In the middle are banks for which fairness and balance are essential and which bend over backwards to achieve equality across the board.

Underpinning the 'our team takes over' approach is a blend of trust in known and tested executives plus operating systems and processes with which the home team is totally familiar. As John Skerritt of Andersen Consulting explains:

If you're talking about a mission critical job, you want loyalty first of all. You want people who will do what they're told whatever the organisation chart says. The new guy [from the acquired bank] has to be demonstrably better – or picked for political reasons.

Inextricably linked with loyalty is knowledge of the systems and processes which will be employed in the merged bank. Executives who have designed and operated systems such as First Union's Future Bank and the former NationsBank's Model Bank understandably have an advantage in the selection process, however meritocratic it may be. As we discuss in the chapter on IT systems, this advantage adds fuel to the technical debate on choice of systems.

Deutsche Bank's Scott Moeller confirms an understandable bias of a dominant acquirer in selecting support professionals:

> The other bank's system may be better in some respects, but in some cases it may not be worth the extra pain to adapt to a slightly better system.

Austin Adams of First Union offers the response of a serial acquirer whose system will be employed in the merged entity:

> I'll look for the best talent. If there's a tie, the tie goes to someone from First Union who can say "I know the system". But all the key positions are in play. We obviously need to build our talent pool. In 1985, we were only a $7 billion bank. We're now at $240 billion, and you clearly need more talent to run that organisation.

Balance and fairness are the key variables for a variety of mergers, particularly those in Europe and Japan whose sponsors feel they must demonstrate that a merger of equals requires equality of senior jobs. In the three-way KBC merger in Belgium involving a mutual insurer, stockholder-owned bank and another mutual bank, the top 18 jobs in the new structure have been allocated equally. Co-heads from the component banks forming Unibank and ABN Amro ensured a fair, albeit complex, representation of all parties to the merger. Roughly half of the new Bank Austria's current top 12 executives served with Creditanstalt, while the top team of MeritaNordbanken was initially composed of equal numbers from each partner. Fairness in banks like ING and ABN Amro is sustained by a tradition of appointing chief executives alternately from the predecessor institutions.

The majority of the banks in our universe, however, have emphasised meritocracy in their choice of top people. A number have used outside consultants or executive recruiters to manage the selection process. For example, HypoVereinsbank made a serious effort to achieve its goal of 'a merger of the best' by setting up an assessment centre manned by bank executives to select talent for jobs below management board level.

Interestingly enough, the banks who scored most heavily in our straw poll of successful mergers – Lloyds TSB and Chase Manhattan – argue most vociferously in favour of a selection process that is, and is seen to be, objective and transparent. Lloyds TSB's selection process is described by Chief Financial Officer Kent Atkinson:

> Getting the right people in the right place is essential for a merger. Even though Lloyds was twice the size of TSB, we decided at the outset not to allocate top jobs in this ratio as our principal objective was to get the best person for the job, irrespective of which bank he/she came from. We cleaned the board: every management job had to be applied for. We required at least one candidate for each job from each of the two banks. Then we had a 'grandfathering' process: each of us had a 'grandfather' from each of the two banks who reviewed our decision. It was a huge machine – very time consuming [it took three–four months] but we tried very hard to get the best material. You never get a 100 per cent result but we did get the best people from both sides. All the staff saw that it was a fair process.

One of the products of the Lloyds TSB merger was the choice of Sir Brian Pitman's successor from TSB, Peter Ellwood. One of our consulting friends involved in the process comments that:

> Sir Brian was supremely indifferent as to where an executive came from. He was even accused by Lloyds people of favouring the other bank.

Walter Shipley's reputation for meritocracy can be traced to his roots as a junior in a bank merger in 1959 when his bank was taken over by the former Chemical Bank:

> It was clear who was being acquired. My role models all left, and the rest of us moped around the corridors wondering whether we had a brand on our backs. The message was clear: we weren't as good as they. Forty years later we see how avoiding prejudice and treating people fairly has worked for us all. I've had to fight against our own people who want to do it 'our way'.

His colleague Mark Garvin confirms the result:

> Walter goes out of his way to be fair and statesmanlike. He sets the
> tone; you feel you have to abide by that ethos of trust. The message is
> transmitted exponentially throughout the organisation.

It is banks like Lloyds TSB, Chase and Wells Fargo aiming at
creating a wholly new institution who are the most articulate advocates
of an open and rigorous people selection process. Each believes that
their scarce resource in the future will be qualified professionals. A
fundamental rationale for their merger is to expand the supply of this
talent. Chase's Garvin articulates the view neatly:

> Success in the future will also be a function of how we build a
> management elite. While none of the three heritage institutions was
> a world-beater, the new Chase is immeasurably superior to its pre-
> decessors. This is because a merger is not just about mechanistic
> implementation but also about creating value through a continuous
> process of transformation into something completely different. If we
> are successful, we will develop an elite of high performers who will be
> prepared to leave if they are not challenged, but willing to stay if we
> create the right culture!

Dick Kovacevich of Wells Fargo agrees that selecting the best people
is an essential merger goal:

> No people decision is perfect, but you have to do your best. This isn't
> a personality contest. Most merging banks don't get it right, which is
> why most mergers don't add value. No two mergers are exactly the
> same, but the fundamentals are. Integrity is so important. You can't
> fake people out!

Lloyds TSB's Atkinson echoes the need to improve the human resource
base:

> Choosing people in a bank merger usually means imposing your own
> people on the other bank. That's the first mistake! You need new
> thinking, not the old heritage, to build a new bank.

John McCoy of Bank One agrees that building the human resource
base is a key merger goal:

My conclusion is that the bigger the banking company, the smarter the people. There's a lot of brainpower; you can't overwhelm them.

The alternative of losing superior talent is painful. Pricewaterhouse Coopers consultant Mark Felman points out that:

> the bright people you do not pick leave with proprietary knowledge of your technology, products and customers. They go to your competitors with revenge in their hearts. They leave behind demoralized colleagues, incomplete products, and a knowledge gap![1]

RETAINING THE BEST AND BRIGHTEST

The centrifugal forces working against retention of key professionals are awesome. The blandishments of headhunters, the pain of uncertainty, the confusion of new bosses and colleagues – all demand a major investment in countervailing measures. And on top of the added preoccupations, bankers have a 'day job' – that of continuing to run a bank – often with their ranks depleted by voluntary and mandated departures. One study describes a merger as:

> an extraordinary and destabilizing life event requiring considerable personal adjustment.[2]

Mark Garvin's description of the challenge is graphic:

> It's a Darwinian struggle – a process of creative destruction.

Faced with this challenge, the consulting fraternity recommends face-to-face communication, the identification of key individuals to be retained and a tailored message for each, and early termination of executives who do not espouse the merger. A leading consulting firm's presentation focuses on over-communication:

> when you are sick and tired of repeating the same messages over and over, you may be starting to get through!

Several consultants emphasise that the chances of retaining the commitment of key professionals in an environment of uncertainty diminishes sharply after the initial 'hundred days'. To improve his success rate, Chase's Shipley emphasises the value of demonstrable and sizeable gains from the merger:

once these mega-gains are demonstrable, employees are far more likely to accept the pain involved in a merger's layoffs and redundancies. By contrast, the authoritarian, "my way" style of mergers can demotivate the staff of the acquired institution.[3]

But the forces militating against meritocracy are powerful. In its earlier investment banking merger with SG Warburg, the former SBC had acquired a reputation as a meritocratic manager of talent. In its merger with UBS, however, a good share of the UBS talent left to take up senior positions with competitors such as ING Barings and Donaldson, Lufkin & Jenrette. CEO Marcel Ospel acknowledges that in selected areas the result was disappointing:

> We knew it would be bloody so we moved quickly to protect the franchise. We told our people to treat the UBS people properly to make them feel at home and extend our talent base. But it came out differently and we lost people we would rather have kept. While we wanted a merger of equals, we came up against a fact of life in investment banking.

Several former UBS executives confirmed their sense of not being wanted in the new organisation. To quote one friend:

> The larger the paycheque, the greater the frustration.

Resentment and a sense of being disenfranchised are often directed at the leadership responsible for the deal who have won top jobs or retention payments from the merger. A former Bankers Trust executive recalls the number of T-shirts circulating in New York with the motto 'Frank Newman [the former CEO] got $100 million and all I got was this lousy T-shirt.'

Another force acting against meritocracy in many markets are staff unions who resist change in general and meritocracy in particular. One friend in a European bank notes that:

> Our CEO really believes in meritocracy. The intent is there, but labour laws, inflexible salary scales, and even our personnel department sometimes impede the implementation of meritocratic decisions.

Other banks take a different view on the value of acquiring new skills. Fleet Bank has won a reputation as an efficient acquirer of other banks, although its merger in 1999 with Bank Boston is by far the largest it has undertaken. Fleet's Brian Moynihan, who managed the merger process, emphasises process over people:

> In a bank merger you have to reduce headcount. The people with the highest compensation, however, are not always necessarily the ones to keep. You need to use the mix that does the trick. You should avoid demoting anyone. A merger is a great opportunity to clean house, since traditionally few bankers have been terminated.

With regard to speed in people decision-making, in Chapter 4 we cited the number of banks which point with pride to their ability to name top management at the same time as the merger is announced publicly. One of the techniques used by several banks to combat this trauma is to move staff from the merging banks physically together in common premises as soon as possible. What Bernard Michel of Credit Agricole terms 'interpenetration' was also recommended by Ignace Temmerman, Managing Director of KBC's CBC affiliate:

> We decided to merge our branch network as soon as possible. As a result we developed some temporary technology solutions and a level of collaboration which wouldn't have happened as rapidly as if we had remained separate.

We found several banks that used the merger as an opportunity to rejuvenate the human resource base. Perhaps the best example is Swedbank, which combined a retirement plan for staff over the age of 57 with the opportunity for all other staff to leave after 18 months of training if they felt they were not in tune with the bank's new vision. A total of 4,000 of the 14,000 pre-merger thus left over the merger period and were partially replaced by new talent. Soren Andersson explains:

> All the staff were given two days of exposure to our new vision. Then they spent two days focusing on what this vision meant for each of them. They were asked if they wanted to stay, and if the answer was 'no' they were offered extensive training to help in job hunting. To build our competence, we also gave several weeks of training to those who stayed – we even had to close branches to make time for the training.

Yet despite these efforts, Swedbank management has acknowledged that staff disruption and customer dissatisfaction have been a significant problem.

One of the major lessons learned by several of our interviewees is to jettison those who do not support the merger goals. In Chapter 4 we described the efforts made by Bernard Michel of Credit Agricole to evaluate the commitment of individual members of his team to the merger with Indosuez. BBV's Luis Bastida agrees:

> Some people are simply not happy after a merger. The sooner they leave the better. It can be pretty costly, but if they're not in tune with the new project they should go. You also need a process to bring conflicts to the surface. They should be addressed as soon as possible rather than pretend they don't exist. A mechanism for conflict resolution is essential in a merger, as some of these conflicts can't be solved in the normal course of business.

One of the issues raised by this analysis is the imperfections inherent in the people selection process. Given the limited time available, as well as the pressures from inside and outside the organisation to select individuals who are not the best and brightest, how can management build a talent base for a more competitive future?

And the corollary question is whether it makes sense at all to incorporate new elements in the talent pool. Are some segments of banking – like retail – simply destined to compete on cost rather than human talent?

8 Cultural Conflict: The Battle for Hearts and Minds

The clash of cultures is a central issue in any bank merger. From whatever background they come, each bank has its own set of values, of 'how we do things around here' and of what behaviour gets rewarded or punished. Addressing this 'soft' issue is a major leadership challenge whose success can only be evaluated over years, if not decades.

In their prescription for merger process, most management consultants recommend explicitly defining these different cultural traits and putting them on the table for open discussion. The challenge of the leadership is to communicate and demonstrate by personal behaviour the values which will characterise the new banking entity in the future. Symbolic acts, such as branding, location of headquarters units, and titles are important. Means of changing behaviour, such as compensation structures and retention payments, also play a key role.

Our survey of over 30 banks reveals the almost universal presence of different cultures in the parties to the merger. Entrepreneurial vs. bureaucratic, centralised vs. decentralised, savings bank vs. stockholder-owned bank, value vs. profit oriented, customer vs. product driven – all add combustible fuel to the uncertainty and anticipation of change triggered by the announcement of a merger. Organisations rooted in the same geography – whether a region such as Bavaria or the US Midwest or a nation state – have developed strong cultural traits which are accentuated in the febrile atmosphere of a traumatic merger.

Our interviewees agree that such differences are indeed universal as well as deeply rooted. Even though roughly half of BCP's top management – including Pedro Libano Monteiro himself – had spent a good portion of their earlier careers with BPA, the cultural differences are sharp. As Monteiro explains:

> The merger went a bit more smoothly as a result, but the cultural differences have still been an important problem. Culture is a problem that you never really solve. Even after 30 years the differences remain – it's like different nationalities. It's a fact of life that has to be managed.

73

One of the negative surprises in the Class of 1990 mergers was the heat generated by conflict between senior executives at Banco Bilbao and Banco Vizcaya. Outside analysts had taken comfort from the fact that many of these executives had been friends since childhood in the Basque region and gone to the same Deusto University in Bilbao. Yet the ferocity of a power struggle had to be resolved finally by the intervention of the Bank of Spain. One of the principal findings of our 1992 study of these mergers – invariably the first transforming merger undertaken by management – was that cultural conflicts had been underestimated. We summarise our conclusions in that volume as follows:

> experience in the US as well as Europe confirms that resistance to change is usually a much more powerful force than originally anticipated – at least by the individuals at the top who create the merger . . . communicating the objectives of the new organization makes vast demands on top management, but there is no substitute if management wishes to combat the centrifugal forces that, in each of the banks interviewed, act to create a 'we and they' atmosphere.[1]

The issue is still relevant years later, as a friend at Citicorp admits with reference to the Travelers' merger:

> It's a lot tougher than we thought.

In BSCH, José Luis del Valle speaks of the difference between Banco Santander's deal-oriented culture and BCH's numbers-oriented value system propagated by CEO Angel Corcostegui. HVB brings together two Bavarian banks – one with an entrepreneurial, risk-oriented bias and the other with a more centralised orientation towards control.

John McCoy points out that both Bank One and First Chicago NBD have strong Mid-west roots and common values of honesty and diligence. Yet it was still felt necessary to bring in an outside consultant to bridge the two banks' cultures:

> Our top 30 people spent a few days together talking about cultural differences. First Chicago had a strong belief in customer service, while Bank One is very profit focused. We talked it out and found we weren't that far apart.

KBC's three-way merger requires integrating a stockholder-owned bank and two mutual institutions. Ignace Temmerman of KBC's CBC affiliate is optimistic:

You can't over-estimate the importance of local culture. It takes a long time, and you should not disturb this local culture but rather integrate the strong characteristics of all partners involved. Be proactive, but allow time for the mayonnaise to set. You definitely need a positive attitude: the glass of water is half full – never half empty! Once convinced of the strategy you need to show a strong belief in the project and communicate it. If you don't believe in your own future, you don't have any!

In Credit Agricole's merger with Banque Indosuez, Bernard Michel notes a host of conflicting value systems:

That merger brought together a number of different orientations: retail vs. corporate, mutualist vs. capitalist, and control vs. risk-taking. But we were all professionals, so that the differences were reconcilable.

Within the merged Citigroup, the cultural differences – particularly as they relate to the strategic objective of cross-selling – are marked. Travelers has developed a highly refined marketing culture built around selling multiple products to its retail customer base, while Citibank's culture is widely known for focus on a given unit's own bottom line. This adds another challenge to an already complex management task. As a friend at Citibank jokes:

Conflict would exist anyway without the merger, which simply makes the conflict more visible. I now hear people at Citibank saying "We don't fight among ourselves any more. We now have a common enemy" [in the Travelers]!

John Tiner of Arthur Andersen notes a sharp difference in cultural profile between US and European banks:

In the US, there's usually a dominant partner who decides *every-thing*. In Europe, the banks *compromise* much more!

The clash between nationalities introduces another source of conflict into the mix of values. MeritaNordbanken, the pioneering cross-border merger in Europe, is fully aware of the challenge. Ari Laakso points out that:

The relationship between Finland and Sweden has never been an easy one. We've always been competitors. The Swedes have always been seen from Finland as the big, rich brother. There's the fear that 'the Swedes are taking over'. But it hasn't happened, as we've worked fast to develop a new corporate culture.

MeritalNordbanken's Chairman, Jacob Palmstierna, agrees that language and culture remain a major issue two years after the merger:

> Finland was a part of Sweden for 700 years. Of course, there are differences, but we say that diversity is our strength. We are working hard to make it just that!

The widespread scepticism over the Deutsche Bank/Bankers Trust fusion stems largely from a perceived culture clash. A former managing director of Bankers Trust expresses a common view:

> There could be a real problem in the future. German military precision and size may well conflict with the Bankers Trust "loosy-goosy" style. There's a lot of resentment about the fat retention payments made to senior people. Will the Bankers Trust people reach out and will Deutsche Bank accept them?

DEALING WITH CULTURAL CHANGE

The challenge for management is thus clear: how to address the clash of values and behaviour?

One solution – that of the decentralised federation – simply avoids the issue for at least several years after the merger. Such diversity is even emphasised as a positive value. Hessel Lindenbergh of ING sings its praises:

> ING has always been able to bring together successfully different institutions. There's lots of value in maintaining local autonomy. We go to great lengths to support local marketing and delivery, with over 30 different brands in the group. We're not interested in imposing rigid guidelines except in areas like risk management where it really matters.

Several other multi-national or multi-business merged entities have essentially left their operating units alone. At Dexia, the product of an 'economic' merger of Belgian and French public sector finance banks, Paul Vanzeveren explains:

We have different but compatible cultures. We foresee a slow process of harmonisation at the operating level and would like to facilitate mobility within the group, but the different regulatory environments pose a real barrier.

Management of Kapital Holding in Denmark takes roughly the same view. The three operating units – a savings bank, payments specialist and mortgage lender – essentially have their own systems and operating identity, and only at the central level is there a common bond.

A second approach is to impose the culture of the dominant entity. Many banks – including some of the most highly regarded – believe deeply that this is the only real solution to cultural conflict. Fleet Boston is one of the most articulate spokesman for this view, as Brian Moynihan explains:

You have to get the culture thing over with as soon as possible. People have to stop thinking about where they came from and focus on where they're going. We tell [a merger partner] 'you *are* different, but we have a job to do'. As for Fleet's culture, we're almost a chameleon. We've absorbed a lot of new people over the last 15 years and have an open mind and lots of discussion. Our own culture has changed, and we've got a lot more talent. We do have our differences, but life goes on.

The Nordic world's most admired bank, Svenska Handelsbanken, has a uniquely decentralised and profit-oriented culture which it has no intention of changing in the merger process. Lars Gronstedt describes the integration of Stadshypotek:

We have a strong culture; it's accepted, and our people are happy with it. We welcomed the Stadshypotek people into our branch network and gave them lots of seminars on Handelsbanken culture. A massive brainwashing, as everyone at Handelsbanken says the same thing! We're unwavering and would never consider a mixing of cultures. Mergers are tough enough without that too! There's an extraordinary focus on profitability. We're a coherent institution; everybody knows what he has to do.

Another well-respected Nordic bank, Den norske Bank, agrees that blending cultures is a major risk. Tom Grondahl explains:

There are two models in the Nordic region: doing very big deals with the risk of cultural conflict and smaller ones which do not impair the culture of the buyer. Den Danske Bank and we belong in the latter camp.

Stung by its experience with the Morgan Grenfell merger in 1989, Deutsche Bank in its GCI corporate and institutions banking unit has imposed its culture on Bankers Trust – but with a difference. The BT merger is being managed by Anglo-Saxon investment banking professionals with a totally different culture from that of the parent bank's other German-based entities. As Scott Moeller points out:

> A majority of the members of the GCI management board have come from the Anglo-Saxon investment banking culture, and only a few are German-born. Deutsche Bank is the only global investment bank that has two significant business divisions [including GCI, which accounts for half of total group profits] headquartered [in London] outside its home country. None of our US competitors can say that.

While meritocracy has driven its people selection process in the TSB merger, Lloyds retains its uniquely powerful commitment to a stockholder-value oriented culture. When asked about cultural integration, Kent Atkinson responds with a description of the conversion of TSB management to Lloyds' way of thinking:

> We held a number of teach-ins for TSB and Cheltenham & Gloucester [the mortgage affiliate] managers on our financial disciplines. TSB had focused on customer satisfaction. It was a long process, but we convinced the ex-TSB management that you can't achieve stockholder value goals with dissatisfied customers: the two must go together.

BUILDING A NEW CULTURE

The third generic category of cultural change is the creation of a new set of values which is notably different from those of the predecessor banks. In their understandable desire to focus their colleagues' attention on the future rather than the past, most of the 'new' values for the merged bank are performance-related. Underpinning this strategy is the assumption that it is behaviour, rather than values, which must be altered. Mark Felman of Pricewaterhouse Coopers puts it bluntly:

> Beliefs are stubborn. Behaviour is flexible. It is easier to try new behaviours than to alter beliefs.[2]

UniCredito is an excellent example of this approach. As Roberto Nicastro explains:

> Our strong focus is on performance. It's always tempting in a post-merger environment to complain about political choices. Having ambitious plans and budgets helps people think about getting their act together. We work from day one in the merger to build a reporting system and use internal benchmarking and peer pressure to achieve the targets. By moving lots of people from back office jobs to selling ones, we've both created a selling culture as well as liberated a lot of them from being a pariah in the back office.

A similar strategy is followed by HVB, a bank struggling with a host of internal and external challenges. Stefan Ermisch emphasises that:

> We're building a performance culture. We've got a long way to go, but when people say 'in the old bank we did it this way' our response it that we are a new bank and the old ones don't exist any more. We still hear people talking about how different it was in a predecessor bank, Bayerische Staatsbank, back in the 1970s!

Erste Bank's Andreas Treichl also articulates a new vision and culture for his merger of a retail and a corporate bank:

> From the beginning we've emphasised that we're a completely new bank – the leading privately-owned large financial institution in the country. Forget the two old banks. If you go through the bank, you'll see that maybe eight out of nine people don't feel the merger at all. We had totally different cultures: GiroCredit had a loose management structure, while Erste was a retail banking machine. The idea of a new bank has helped a lot in the merger process.

Setting and achieving performance goals is not the only value being injected into the new culture. A host of others – customer service,

integrity, collaboration, innovation and client orientation – are fea-
tured more in marketing documents and client presentations than
actual practice, but in a few cases the bank's leadership has truly
integrated some of these ideals. As indicated in earlier chapters,
Chase Manhattan is one of these institutions which has truly under-
gone a cultural transformation with its focus on meritocracy, fairness
and trust. Walter Shipley explains how this has been done:

> The principal lesson of experience is the critical importance of creat-
> ing a win – win environment. We inherited lots of cultural luggage
> [from the three predecessor banks]. With ManHan we quickly
> conveyed the view that the new company was better than the old
> one. We showed respect and honour for the history of both of our
> merger partners. We got people focusing forward, not backward. All
> of us have a tendency to look backward. We don't like change and
> we're creatures of habit. And people look at the negative aspects of
> change.
>
> But my peers and I had been CEOs long enough so that we didn't
> need our egos stroked; we didn't compete between ourselves for
> glory. At the top [in both mergers] we created a partnership and
> articulated the model to the rest of the bank. We believed in the
> power of human leverage, which creates tremendous value. We've
> come a long way since the dark days of the 1970s, and people are
> proud of the record. Success breeds success. People believe it's a
> meritocracy and an attractive place to work. The new bank is so
> much better than its predecessors.

Another bank which has focused successfully on 'soft' values is the
new Wells Fargo. Dick Kovacevich's challenge is to blend such a 'high
touch' culture from the old Norwest with the 'high tech' values of the
former Wells Fargo:

> You need to have agreement before the merger in sufficient detail on
> philosophy. Our value statement tells everyone what we believe in.
> We've taken the best from both banks – the old Wells' Internet and
> supermarket banking capability and much of Norwest's traditional
> stores [branches] and approach to community banking. In the merger
> process we asked the heads of function from each bank to tell us
> what makes sense. If they can't agree, we [the four members of the
> office of the Chairman] will break the tie. And we've had only a few
> minor disagreements.

Another CEO who is deeply concerned about building a new culture is Unibank's Thorleif Krarup. Having arrived on the scene in a time of cultural and financial turmoil, he makes an interesting distinction between hard and soft issues:

> You must act quickly on hard decisions but take your time on the soft issues. You can't establish a set of corporate principles on day one and chase people around if they don't behave accordingly. Top management's challenge is to establish this single set of values but it takes years of dialogue. We started the process in 1994 and agreed a statement of direction three years later. Now we're broadening it to assess each individual leader.

A final comment on cultural differences is provided by Phil Ryan, CFO and member of the group executive board of Credit Suisse Group and who is a former investment banker specialising in financial institutions, with a deep knowledge of the merger process. In his view:

> The scariest thing is to be at a banking conference and hear two CEOs of merging banks get up and say 'we have two great banks with the same culture'. For me that sends off alarm bells. What they should be saying is that 'we're very different and one of us is in charge'. It's the people who acknowledge that they're different who are the most successful in the long run.

Two similar cultures can indeed generate more conflict than different ones. As Cartwright and Cooper point out in their volume on mergers, two dominant cultures will be at each other's throats as they seek to exercise their primacy, while the fusion of a dominant and a laid back or passive one can be a recipe for success.[3]

Our findings in this chapter raise several questions which we shall address in the final chapter. First, how successful has bank leadership been in actually achieving a new culture with well-implanted new values. Is there more smoke than fire? And secondly, should cultural change be introduced immediately or after the dust has settled on the fusion process?

9 IT Decisions: Everybody's Problem!

The selection of IT (information technology) systems and the subsequent conversion process to common platforms rank high on the list of issues which continue to frustrate bank mergers. It was this issue which caused the brow of most of our bank interviewees to furrow and elicited tales of frustration, conflict, unexpected costs and delays. It is thus not surprising that the post-merger integration manuals of the leading consulting firms devote, to the untutored generalist, more space to this topic than any other merger issue. The reasons for this preoccupation are not hard to find.

- *IT investment involves big money – both incremental investment and potential savings.* A McKinsey & Co. presentation concludes that 30–50 per cent of all bank merger synergies depend directly on IT and that up to 25 per cent of IT costs can be saved in bank mergers. IT spending overall accounts for an estimated 15–20 per cent of banks' total costs and is growing at a similar annual rate as banks update legacy systems and invest in new products and distribution channels. As we shall discuss below, cost overruns on IT projects can be substantial, and the write-offs on major projects concealed in a bank's aggregate cost figures can be equally alarming.
- *The IT selection and conversion process effectively drives the merger timetable.* Typically the process ends with the final conversion of the merged bank's core retail system. Most cost savings from branch closures and reduction in IT staff and spending are thus tied to this schedule, and any delay in the process can be a costly one from the standpoint of stockholder value. In our research we found a remarkably wide range of total time spans for IT integration, ranging from as short as six months to six years. Clearly the technical nature of the task to a large extent drives this timetable, but one suspects that completion dates have often in practice lagged the original time line.
- *For most banks the selection of major systems – in particular the core retail platform – is an immensely complex one from a technical standpoint.* In Europe, for example, virtually every major bank

possesses a patchwork of so-called legacy systems, generally developed in-house over a period of several decades, which is almost universally condemned as outdated, costly to run and inadequate in its functionality. By any standard, reaching a decision on the way forward is a challenging one. US banks have made more progress in using standard packages and outsourcing key functions, but the systems decision can still be a challenging one.

- *This technical decision is complicated immensely by subjective and human considerations.* As the systems have often been developed in-house by the team which now runs them, egos as well as jobs are at stake. The decision to use 'our' system rather than 'theirs' for professional staff can mean the difference between, on the one hand, being out of a job, and on the other, the master of a much larger and more expensive IT function. As indicated in Chapter 7, other things being equal, when one bank's system is chosen over another's, the staff of the former may be more likely to be asked to stay on.

- *The selection of 'our' system is also a badge of honour in the balancing act which weighs perceived winners and losers in the merger process.* Quite apart from the technical merits or demerits of a given IT system, the ability to claim ownership of at least the core of the platform chosen can be a reward for losses elsewhere in the balance of advantage or a confirmation of dominance as an overall winner in the merger sweepstakes.

- *Finally, big IT projects – in particular the development of major new systems – can be complex and massive ones, and banks in general have not covered themselves with glory in managing such projects.* In an earlier book,[1] we explored the reasons why even the best-managed banks stumble over this challenge. Lack of interest and understanding by top management in IT in general, stop-go investment policies geared to current earnings rather than long-term technology needs, and the lack of the requisite specialist skills all play a role.

Given the level of concern expressed by our bank interviewees on this topic, we made a particular effort to glean the findings and conclusions of the leading IT and management consulting firms who have played an important role in assisting banks with their IT decisions. Their views are remarkably consistent, so we summarise many of them before turning to the results of our bank interview series.

MAKING A MEAL OUT OF INFORMATION TECHNOLOGY (IT) DECISIONS

A key observation made by virtually all of the consulting firms we met is that banks tend to spend an inordinate amount of time on key IT decisions. A corollary is that this effort produces compromises which, in turn, usually increase the cost and complexity of the final product. One of the early choices in the integration process is whether to have the IT dimension run by a committee of interested executives or a single project manager empowered to make decisions without reference to anyone except to the CEO or executive committee. John Skerritt of Andersen Consulting is quite specific on his preference:

> You have to use an 800-pound gorilla of a project manager rather than a committee. He should have unquestioned authority [subject to the CEO's approval] to take any decision on the merger process. A steering committee just can't do the job. There is a relative lack of CEOs willing to dominate the process, and what you often get is a collegiate process which tends to fudge the tough decisions. Overall, you need an extremely strong central programme management with a tightly integrated programme which brings together IT and other functions and works on a critical path. You can't let it become diffuse.

More specifically, our friends at McKinsey and similar firms place key IT systems decisions within the first portion of the famous 100 days. In other words, during the first month or so following the merger decision, the basic platforms should be selected.

A related issue is that of compromise over the elements of these core systems. The consensus of the consultants is not to cherry-pick between basic technologies – a favourite compromise of bankers in a merger of equals environment. Nick Viner of BCG explains:

> The worst thing you can do is to try to take the best of each side. It's almost as bad as starting afresh and will probably take years to implement. Each system is likely to have a different functionality. Inevitably in a merger you'll lose some of that functionality. You need to be pragmatic and make trade-offs.

Diogo Teixera of the Tower Group, an IT specialist, agrees:

> The issue is not technology but functionality – what the system does as opposed to what the client wants. No matter what you do in a

merger, someone's going to lose features of his functionality. It's human nature. If you take a feature away from someone, no matter how trivial, there's someone who's going to complain.

Particularly in Europe, where the use of third party packages is less prevalent than in the US, the problems posed by legacy systems are immensely complicated. As John Rolander of Gemini explains:

In Europe, the situation in a bank merger is usually the following: 'I've got my legacy system, you've got yours, and they're both albatrosses'. What's critical is a common architecture, which doesn't usually exist, so you can use plug and play solutions, outsourcing, and middleware. And there's no competitive advantage in writing your own code!

John Tiner, head of Arthur Andersen's banking practice, expresses the same view:

In Europe there are more compromises on everything! You have disparate systems, no common architecture and short-term compromises are not sustainable. So you have to look at a common platform with intelligent middleware and plug-and-play components – essentially component-based architecture. The cost of integrating the existing systems can be greater than the cost of new software. The people who do this best are the major US investment banks.

The final warning of the consultants is against building the comprehensive long-term IT solution which may be recommended by in-house IT teams confronted by these legacy problems. As Norman Bernard of First Consulting suggests:

If you give the IT management the opportunity [to build a new system], they'll make a meal of it and you find yourself with a five-year project. IT people can be tyrants and hold the CEO to ransom.

Most of the lessons of IT experience expressed by our banker universe reflect these views.

Perhaps the dominant lesson is that top management must make – and sustain – simple and crisp high-level decisions on IT. Walter Shipley of Chase, who has been through this process twice during the past decade, explains:

In the ManHan/Chemical merger, we made the mistake of picking every sub-component based on a detailed evaluation; it took much too much time. For the Chase merger, we concentrated on families of systems – a much easier process.

One of these high-level decisions may be to jettison an expensive system which has just been, or is about to be, installed by one of the merging banks. Several of our banks made this painful decision during their more recent round of mergers. Thus Danilo Melamed of Bank Austria admits that:

> This time [for the Creditanstalt merger] we were more clever. We chose one of the two banks' systems and threw the other away. Last time [for the Z Bank merger] we were 'consulted' into a mix which kept both alive and linked together. It was too complex, too expensive and never completed. This time Creditanstalt had a new system which saved us the development cost. But it still took us a year to make the decision because we wanted to reach a consensus. It was amazing even then to see how many 'counter revolutionaries' there are who want to revisit the decision. So management had to say 'we don't discuss it any more – it's decided'.

Another painful decision was made by the management of BSCH when comparing the system being developed by Banco Santander compared with that in operation at BCH. Matias Inciarte of BSCH, who had been deeply involved at Santander in designing its system, summarises their experience:

> It took us a few months this time to decide on a single platform – that of BCH. Every effort we made to compromise between the two produced a higher cost. We kept saying 'let's tweak this a bit' or "let's try to mix and match". But that's the worst of all possible worlds.

A UNIVERSAL PROBLEM

But the core system choice can be a much tougher one. BBV chose the route in its 1988 merger of equals to build a brand-new system. Internal debate plus the time necessary to build from scratch extended the merger period into the mid-1990s. As Luis Bastida explains, however, that may have been the best possible outcome:

In 1988 the technology was changing. The client server was state of the art but there were only a few applications by a major bank. Rather than choose one of the two existing systems, we decided to instal a totally new one across the bank. Big projects take more time, and we had to support three different systems for a time. But now we have a great competitive advantage and are a retail leader as a result. Over a ten-year time frame it was the right decision.

Bank One has also had its share of frustration with major systems. Having decided to convert in the mid-1990s to a single platform for its formerly decentralised network, the bank is still struggling to install a common platform. John McCoy vents his frustration:

> I've made a lot of mistakes at Bank One but the worst was to let each of the banks we bought keep their own system. We should have gone to a common platform much earlier. We're desperately trying to get to one set of common systems and are installing them one bank at a time. In one state, we had a heated discussion with our commercial bankers who wanted their own system. It took us six months to say 'no'! You need to be rational. Our Internet bank, Wingspan, was up and running in only four months with its own system! In my career, we've tried to build from scratch two new systems, and in each case we found that the technology changed faster than we could write the software.

Even the highly regarded Wells Fargo team has had to struggle with its IT decisions. In the words of Dick Kovacevich:

> We made the decision in the most complex way possible. It would have been a lot faster to flip a coin and take one of the two, and only one half of the bank would have had to change. But sizeability was an issue, and we ended up taking the best of both and essentially a brand-new system. There's a high cost in the short term and a three-year merger period as a result, but two plus two should equal five in the long term!

The internal dialogue on IT solutions has been a source of frustration with a number of the banks interviewed. Bernard Michel of Credit Agricole describes his analysis of the appropriate systems to use in the merger with Indosuez:

I kept being told that the two sides couldn't agree because of IT problems. It almost sank the boat! In some business lines, they suggested building a new system. I had to get involved myself to study the situation. The choice was complex but my decision – to select the biggest or the most efficient one to minimise disruption – has worked well. The lesson for me is that 'an IT problem' is a justification for resistance to the merger, and I almost fell into the trap.

A number of interviewees opined that agreeing the final IT solution has taken more effort and expense than might have been absolutely necessary from a technical standpoint. Thus Wilco ten Berg of ABN Amro acknowledges that:

We selected from both ABN and Amro. It was a compromise, and most of the IT people were happy. We could have been more rigorous, and it cost a bit of money.

Roberto Nicastro describes the complex process of designing the all-important core banking system for UniCredito's federal banking model:

For the first common system [in Rolo Banca] we took a patchwork approach after months of analysis – about one-third each from Rolo and Credito Italiano and one-third new. For the UniCredito merger we have mainly relied on the Credito platform but given IT leadership to the people of Cariverona who had a distinct cultural edge in this area.

Using outside consultants is often a critical factor in reaching a decision on core banking systems, especially when the internal experts cannot agree or may not have the necessary expertise. Kent Atkinson of Lloyds TSB describes a situation similar to that profiled above by John Rolander:

Both banks built their platforms over 20 years ago. They worked but were held together with rubber bands and sticky tape. We wanted one platform for our combined customer base, and it was clear that neither existing system could do it. We used outside consultants to get an objective view.

For the US banks which have invested heavily recently in a single, scalable system capable of handling substantial volume from new acquisitions, the challenge is less daunting. Fleet Boston's Brian Moynihan explains:

> There's very little to do except to move people to our platform because our core bank is much larger. If one system is dominant, you usually convert to it. The cost of training people to move to a smaller system usually rules that out. IT can become a religious debate; 98 per cent of what a system does is standard – the rest is bells and whistles. We've picked up things from all our bank acquisitions but for the core deposit system there's no debate. There can be subtleties but there's no silver bullet – it's just retail banking. Get the conversion done, and the functionality later.

First Union's Austin Adams describes his philosophy of systems integration:

> There are two key variables: the quality of your people and the crispness of the decision-making process. Having singularity in application systems drives everything. We have a decision- making matrix on one page with three columns for each key decision: who will make it, who can have input to the decision, and the individual responsible for recommending the decision. All of these decisions are made during the first month of the merger process, with a date for each. The key decision is the product line; lots of energy is spent on that, with a debate between marketing, product and systems people. If those decisions can't be made on a timely basis, the whole timetable falls apart.

To an outside analyst, one the biggest unknowns in evaluating potential systems problems is the extent of possible conversion problems. Quite apart from the aggressive timetable and staffing which lay behind the Core States and Wells Fargo/First Interstate disasters, there is the problem of multiple conversion stemming from uncompleted prior mergers. Thus First Union's problems with the Core States conversion were compounded because Core States itself had not converted accounts from its recent significant acquisition of Meridian Bank. Not only did that generate a problem of multiple conversion, but also it required a significant – and unexpected – charge-off in First Union's accounts. In a market characterised by multiple mergers, this could be a significant problem for the future.

IT decisions have played a central role in driving a number of banks into a decision to merge. One of the best-known such case studies is the

Figure 9.1 Hypothetical IT cost saves via acquisitions

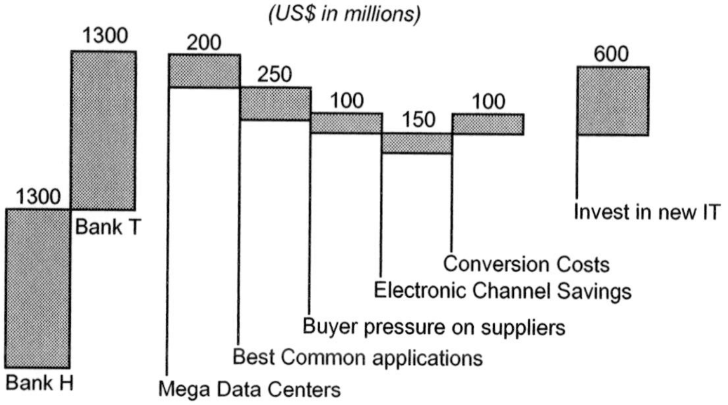

Source: Warburg Dillon Read LLC, The Tower Group.

old Bank of America's decision to seek a merger with Nationsbank. B of A's David Coulter speaks frankly of his dilemma:

I would have been thrilled just to step back and have the world stand still while we improved our quality of service. But the world's not standing still. If you have only a few strategic options, it's better to act than wait.[2]

Figure 9.1 profiles the IT cost saves – and possible new spending – for a typical US bank merger.

Economies can thus be achieved by combining forces, yet these savings can easily be offset by conversion costs and new investment spending.

THE ISSUE OF TIMING

One of the toughest IT issues to resolve is when to make the massive investment to combine major systems – particularly the retail bank. We discussed above the belated decision by Bank One to instal a common retail platform. Banco Santander waited until several years after the acquisition of Banesto, another large retail institution operating under its own brand, before starting to develop a new platform for both banks. We understand that considerable savings could have made by moving earlier rather than operate and develop two separate platforms.

Another European bank delayed IT integration for several years following its 1991 merger. Its CFO explains:

> We didn't even have a single IT function until 1994, three years after the merger. The original federation model was a very inefficient one, and in 1998 we finally integrated the retail banks and started to build a common system. The big issue is whether we could have done this earlier.

Interestingly enough, in the case of Citigroup a merger has actually driven the combined group away from the presumed economies of combined platforms. We understand that plans by the former Citibank to move towards combined platforms for their core consumer and corporate businesses were shelved because of the view from Travelers management that decentralised clusters of technology would promote a more successful entrepreneurial culture.

Looking to the future, a number of the banks in our universe have yet to embark on such a major investment. Following its decision in 1999 to reorganise on a line of business basis, Fortis will be going through the process of systems selection from its component banks. Erste Bank will proceed with a new system when specifications are agreed with the independent savings banks which will share the system.

MeritaNordbanken will eventually have the challenging task of designing a system which is relevant for both the Swedish and Finnish markets. And ING and perhaps Dexia and BG Bank as well in the long term will probably be driven by cost pressures to follow suit. And eventually the leading Japanese banks will follow at their own speed.

The good news is that European banks such as BCP have successfully developed a common system which underpins several different brands and distribution channels. BCP has become a role model for success with its ServiBanca platform built after the acquisition of BPA. Pedro Libano Monteiro points with pride to the result:

> Building ServiBanca was not a problem. We took best practice – largely from BCP – and set up a common platform in two years which services both BCP and BPA with total circularity: the two networks are fully integrated.

It is clear that IT issues will continue to preoccupy bank management. When to convert to common systems will remain an open question as investment costs are measured against those of running and developing duplicate platforms. The technical and subjective trade-offs of systems selection within a merged bank will continue to bedevil management, particularly in Europe and Japan. Arguably the trends toward package solutions, common architecture and outsourcing will facilitate IT decisions. Yet the overarching issue, in our view, is achieving a crisp and timely decision making process.

We address this and other IT issues in our final chapter.

10 The Bank Merger Score Card

What is the bottom line from this in-depth analysis of over 30 specific bank mergers? Can we generalise on the extent to which they have achieved their objectives, whether strategic positioning or specific cost targets? At a minimum, if we accept the academic conclusion that most mergers do not add measurable value, can we prioritise and segment the reasons why they do not?

LIMITED HARD EVIDENCE

Our first conclusion is that a comprehensive statistical analysis of the only hard data – the financial objectives or cost savings – is not likely to prove very satisfying. Such efforts run up against the same constraints of any attempt in a highly complex business to correlate specific causal factors with aggregate financial results. To track the impact of a specific merger over the relevant period of perhaps four years in a large banking institution competing in a changing business environment is extraordinarily difficult at best.

The reasons are clear. In the first place, the data itself is hard to track. Even the banks themselves rarely keep a 'merger P and L' for a long enough period to validate any hard analysis. We cite below a few such cases from our interview series, and we generalise on a number of key variables, but aggregate analysis is not likely to be productive. Conversations with 'serial merger' banks like Bank One and First Union, whose experience would be particularly interesting, confirm that even they do not attempt to track the financial results of a particular transaction.

Secondly, external factors intervene during the merger period. The banking crisis in Norway and Denmark in the early 1990s transformed the business environment for banks like Den Norske and Unibank and threw revenue and cost calculations out the window. Curiously, however, in both these cases the external crisis actually reinforced efforts to implement the merger by cutting costs and bringing different cultures together to save the sinking ship. Thus Nis Obling of Unibank points out that:

We became one bank. We had to stand together, as the life of the bank was at stake.

Tom Grondahl of Den norske Bank agrees:

The banking crisis gave us a lot of motivation to cut costs. We call it the 'invisible hand of the banking crisis'. It would be a lot harder to do it today.

A related form of external change across the US and Europe has been losses from credit and market risk which derailed earnings forecasts and distracted management from merger targets. Severe real estate and other losses from the former East Germany have not only transformed bottom-line results for banks like Bankgesellschaft Berlin and HBV but also helped to poison the merger environment by aggravating the 'we and they' syndrome. In Spain, mounting credit losses also created significant losses and diverted management attention in banks like the former BCH, Argentaria and BBV. The Asian banking crisis in 1997 and the Russian default in 1998 threw the projections of banks like Credit Agricole Indosuez off track.

While the US banks generally avoided such unexpected losses during the period, the repetition of serial mergers for banks like First Union and Fleet Boston made virtually impossible the tracking of the results of a single transaction.

Finally, a number of banks are reluctant or simply unable to disclose some of the less appetising results of a merger. In our chapter on due diligence we mentioned a number of instances of losses which were neither detected by due diligence nor disclosed specifically in subsequent financial reports. Overruns or write-offs from major IT projects, the loss of business from departing clients or key professionals, and failure to achieve specific cost or revenue targets rarely get reported in the financial press. Thus the incremental cost to Swedbank in its 1997 merger of the payoffs made to older staff and the subsequent expense of re-hiring some of them to fill key jobs has been lumped together with a host of other expense items.

One of the few banks in our sample which did carry out an ex-post review of projected cost savings is BCP in Portugal. Pedro Libano Monteiro reports that such a review confirmed that about 80 per cent of the anticipated cost saves from the BPA merger were achieved, with the shortfall accounted for by unanticipated increases in unit costs. This anecdotal evidence supports research by some of our consulting friends which indicates a similar level of achievement for other bank mergers.

A particularly difficult variable to quantify is the actual loss of market share which could be attributable to the merger. As we indicated in Chapter 3, banks typically project revenue losses of perhaps 5–10 per cent of client volumes depending on the profile of the merger. Statistical analyses carried out by our consulting friends indicates that, within our universe, Unibank and BBV in particular suffered double-digit losses in their revenue base.

Banks are understandably shy in revealing or confirming such losses, and in our conversations with some of these banks in our universe little indication was given of the actual market share figures. Yet revenue and market share loss must be a key variable in the merger formula. We discussed earlier the traumatic impact of losing well over 10 per cent of customer volume in the cases of the Wells/First Interstate and First Union/Core States mergers. Tom Grondahl of Den norske Bank, which is embarking on a major retail merger with Postbanken, articulates a typical view:

> The moment the transaction is announced, the organisation slows down and you start losing market share.

BUT A FEW CONCLUSIONS

But it is possible to draw some general conclusions from the experience of our bank universe.

First, inadequate due diligence has seriously impaired the financial results of a number of mergers. Whether a better job could have been done or whether the merger would have proceeded in any case is another issue. But mergers such as SBC/UBS, Bankgesellschaft Berlin, and HVB have inherited serious – essentially multi-billion-dollar – problems from predecessor banks which have jeopardised, at least in the near term, the overall success of their merger. Banks like Erste and BCP have also written off relatively smaller but still significant inheritances from their merger partner.

Second, only a few banks in our universe who set financial as well as strategic targets would appear to have achieved total success in all their merger objectives. Not surprisingly, essentially all of the merged banks can claim to have achieved their key strategic goals – if only because the merger has been completed and the relevant size-driven goals automatically attained. While a number of bank mergers in Europe and the US announced during the 1990s – such as Bankgesellschaft Berlin and Norddeutsche Landesbank as well as the marriage of Christiania Bank and the insurer Storebrand – were not completed for various reasons, we cannot recall in recent years a case of a major completed merger being undone.

As indicated in Chapter 2, only two-thirds of our sample in the Appendix have set merger-related financial targets of any kind, and in many cases these targets are aggregate goals, such as overall ROE performance, which can be achieved – or not – through a variety of means including the merger itself. And many others within this segment are too young to be evaluated because of the relatively recent date of the merger.

Of the remaining 15 mature mergers with quantified financial targets, perhaps six can be said to have achieved all their declared financial goals: BCP, Chase Manhattan, Den Danske Bank, Unibank, Lloyds TSB, and Svenska Handelsbanken. Of this group, only Chase set both cost and aggregated profitability (ROE) goals for the merged institution. BCP's goal of ROE on incremental capital invested in the acquisition can be assumed to have been met, although we do not have the data needed to verify it. All the others articulated only cost-related saves, and within this group are two banks – Den Danske and Unibank – whose bottom lines suffered severely from the Nordic banking crisis.

The remaining nine have seen their forecasts thrown seriously off course by a variety of events, largely credit and market risk related. BBV, the original Bank Austria merger, HBV, Credit Agricole Indosuez and UBS were derailed by risk-related problems, while First Union and Bank One have suffered, respectively, from merger execution and revenue-related failures. ABN Amro achieved all of its financial targets except the cost/income ratio, while Swedbank also suffered from a ballooning cost/income ratio.

A key conclusion from the above analysis is that many merger goals, such as cost saves, can be achieved while, concurrently, aggregate profitability targets are undermined by unrelated 'bumps on the road' driven by the external environment. This could well be a major explanation of research showing the dominance of merger 'failures' as measured by pre and post-merger financial and stock price performance. Thus the merger itself might justifiably be viewed by management as successful in achieving its targeted financial goals, but the market's overall negative appraisal is correctly driven by aggregate bottom-line results which do not meet investor expectations.

A third observation is that bad execution as well as post-merger problems have had a devastating impact on the stock price and, in some cases, the independence of the merged entity. The stock market has severely punished a number of banks with perceived merger problems by a stock price which has plummeted by one-third or more. In a marketplace where the value of one's paper is central to the success of a merger programme, this can savage a bank's strategy.

Thus in the US, in 1991 Nationsbank acquired a merged Sovran/ C&S entity wounded by management conflict and major IT problems. First Union and the old Wells Fargo were punished in 1998–99 for poor execution of major mergers, while Bank One in 1999 suffered from weakness in its credit card operation acquired in 1997. In Europe, UBS and Swedbank are among those whose stock suffered substantially in the marketplace from perceived post-merger problems. For banks like Bank One and First Union whose stock has also fallen dramatically, their merger programme has had to be shelved until their stock price recovers sufficiently.

In a market environment quick to identify losers who might be acquired profitably by potential winners in the merger game, a bank's independence can be at stake, and the subsequent take-over of Wells Fargo by Norwest is widely cited as a case in point.

On a broader scale, bank stock prices in the US and Europe measured against broad market averages have fallen sharply since their peak in 1998. Figure 10.1 graphically illustrates the sharp relative upturn, for example, in the Euro zone, and subsequent collapse.

Figure 10.1 Euro-zone banking sector relative stock performance 1995–2000

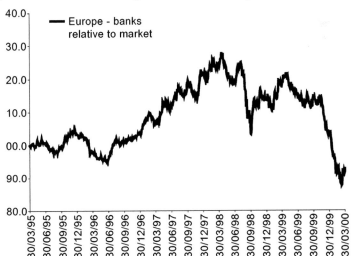

Source: Nomura International Research.

One interpretation of this rise and fall during the late 1990s is the euphoria over bank consolidation, followed by a more realistic interpretation of merger gains and losses. Our conversations with bank stock analysts support this view. The fundamentals of banking have not significantly changed over the period under review: a business with significant overcapacity, modest organic revenue growth, the need to invest heavily in technology, and increasingly threatened by non-traditional competitors. On this reading, the principal justification for the outperformance since 1997 has been the expectation that, individually and collectively, mergers will add stockholder value in banking. A more sober view arguably took hold in late 1998 and 1999.

A fourth observation is that, in many cases, the advertised savings can be dwarfed by the unquantifiable costs of a merger. Low morale, the 'we and they' dichotomy which generates so many political machinations, the amount of time spent at the water cooler exchanging merger gossip rather than servicing customers, the diversion of top management time and attention, the unwanted departure of key professionals attracted by the siren songs of head-hunters – all generate costs which should be mentally deducted from projected merger gains.

In our interviews for this book as well as earlier bank merger studies, we have been impressed by the extent to which management has underestimated the cultural conflict and disruption of a merger and the consequent need to divert management time to repairing the damage. The cost of such disruption cannot be estimated accurately, but it is particularly painful when the quantifiable merger savings are relatively modest.

Another finding constitutes the good news: most banks have eventually emerged from the merger process with their strategic goals achieved. In the European 'Class of 1990', for example, banks like BBV, BCH, and Unibank initially lost market share, suffered cost overruns and experienced significant management turmoil and change, but at the end of the day emerged with a significantly improved market position. The relevant phrase is 'end of the day', as the period of merger disruption was considerably longer than that anticipated. If stockholder value is measured by the present value of future incremental earnings, it is difficult to conclude for many European banks that the merger created much value during that period. Thus, for example, it took perhaps seven years for BBV's key cost/income ratio to return to pre-merger levels.

As Marcel Ospel and others have pointed out, the relevant question might be 'what was the alternative?' By definition we cannot know the answer, but it might well have been a take-over by another bank, or effective marginalisation, with uncertain impact on stockholder value.

In 1996, we carried out a study of seven European banks which had recently undertaken mega-mergers. We concluded that:

> in strategic terms, they did achieve their objectives; they built market share, broadened their business base and avoided the perceived threat of being marginalized in a consolidating marketplace. In financial terms, targets, by and large, were achieved. Yet the targets were, admittedly, modest in terms of potential economies. The 10–15% combined staff and branch capacity savings for a typical European in-market merger is a fraction of what a US bank pairing would have achieved (over the same time period).[1]

A sixth finding is that, as indicated above, unforeseen events have often impaired anticipated merger performance. At Kapital Holding, Gert Kristensen points out that the value to Bikuben of the merger with GiroBank, whose profits as a payments vehicle are driven in large part by cash float, suffered from an unanticipated fall in interest rates following the merger. More common is an economic recession with its impact on asset quality. Banks like BCH and Argentaria in Spain were particularly vulnerable to the severe rise in bad loans as they traversed the critical merger period. In Belgium, a dissident group of Cera stockholders in late 1999 won a court ruling on the issue of valuation and ordered an intermediate holding company in the KBC Group to pay € 2.5 billion to the plaintiffs. While this is not the final word, it is another example of the unexpected 'bumps on the road' in the merger process.

Another unforeseen – but perhaps increasingly predictable – event is the countermoves of competitors to one's merger. Thus ABN Amro's revenue projections were thrown off in the early 1990s by the aggressive response of its Dutch rivals. In 1999, Société Générale's friendly merger with Paribas in France was unexpectedly challenged by Banque Nationale de Paris, which ultimately carried off Société Générale's partner.

And finally, political forces have been unleashed by merger initiatives in Canada, Australia and European countries like Italy, Norway, France and Portugal to forestall take-overs deemed undesirable by governmental and other constituencies. In recent years, UniCredito's proposed merger with Banca Commerciale Italiana, MeritaNordbanken's bid for Christiania and BSCH's bid for Mundial in Portugal have all been derailed or significantly modified by the resistance of local governments and regulators.

A piece of good news is that bank management is becoming more adept at managing the merger process. In much of the literature and in many of our conversations with management consultants, it is pointed out that only a fraction of bank top management has had any experience with the trauma and complexity of a major merger. That profile is changing rapidly in the US and Europe as the merger wave flows on. One after another of our European interviewees, for example, pointed out how much they had learned from their first merger – usually as a member of the 'Class of 1990' – which will enable them to do better in the current round.

11 Case Studies: Specific Lessons for the Future

From our universe of 33 bank mergers, we have selected eight which we view as particularly useful for the lessons they portray – both good and bad. Our selection includes two mergers which have been universally acclaimed as successful, as well as several which appeared at the outset to be marriages made in bank heaven but which have since encountered serious 'bumps on the road'. A fifth is ploughing new ground as an early cross-border merger, and another has sadly become a role model for poor execution. A seventh embodies the new model of a conglomerate growing by acquisition and now abandoning the federal model for an integrated one, and the last reflects what many observers view as the new paradigm in US bank mergers.

The starting point for this selection was a straw poll we conducted with each of our interviewees, both bank executives and consultants, to identify those mergers in the US and Europe regarded as particularly successful. Rightly or wrongly, we felt that such a query for Japan would be premature. We had also thought of ranking the least successful, but did not pursue this rigorously after a consensus quickly emerged. We found a wide range of knowledge of experience of mergers outside the individual banker's home market. Most European and Japanese bankers were comfortable in naming one or more banks outside their national market, with several having actually benchmarked themselves against perceived role models abroad. Interestingly, Lloyds TSB benchmarks itself against Wells Fargo, both the 'old' and 'new' models. On the other hand, some European bankers could focus only on peers in their own national market and therefore disqualified themselves from the poll. In the US, the names of other US banks as good and bad case studies came quickly to mind for virtually all of our interviewees.

This straw poll is only valid as a rough estimate of current sentiment and can in no way form the basis of analytical conclusions. As we point out in the final chapter, role models come and go in banking with uncomfortable rapidity. Yet the widespread consensus among our universe justifies profiling two of these banks – Chase Manhattan and Lloyds TSB – as case studies of perceived merger excellence. We recorded all votes, including multiple mentions, in answer to our question 'who do you think is particularly successful in executing a major merger?'

Among the US banks, of the 14 votes cast, Chase Manhattan accumulated six votes as a successful merger case study, followed closely by the former NationsBank (now Bank of America) with five. The next candidate, with two votes, was the former Norwest (now Wells Fargo). In the European market, of the 23 votes cast, the clear winner was Lloyds TSB with 11 mentions, followed by MeritaNordbanken with four. The HSBC/Midland and ABN Amro mergers each accumulated two votes.

On the basis of this poll of perceived winners plus our own subjective judgement as consultants, we selected for profiling Lloyds TSB, MeritaNordbanken, Chase Manhattan, and the new Wells Fargo. Sadly, we were unable to interview and therefore profile Bank of America for this book.

In addition, we profile UBS and HypoVereinsbank in Europe and First Union in the US who have had to deal with major problems stemming from their mergers. Finally, we analyse Fortis as an example of the multi-product, multi-national federation formed in the 'Class of 1990' but now evolving towards a more integrated model.

A business and strategic profile of each of these institutions is provided in the Appendix along with the other banks interviewed. Our analysis below focuses on their approach to major mergers and the lessons which can be derived from their experience for the future.

MERITANORDBANKEN: THE FIRST FULLY INTEGRATED MAJOR CROSS-BORDER BANK MERGER

While a multitude of banks have acquired financial institutions in other national markets, not until the 1997 fusion of a major Swedish retail bank with Finland's dominant universal bank was such a merger undertaken with the goal of creating not only a true cross-border merger of equals, but also a fully integrated management team at the outset. Given the widespread assumption – as indicated in Chapter 12 – that such cross-border mergers are the wave of the future at least in Europe, much attention has understandably been focused on Merita-Nordbanken as the first of a new banking species. The ranking of MeritaNordbanken in our straw poll is some indication of this interest as well as the perception that the merger is on track.

From the outset, management made it clear that this was a strategic move to create a totally new entity as opposed to a cost-cutting model.

Chief Executive Hans Dalborg stated in the bank's 1998 Annual Report that:

> This is a merger for growth between equal and complementary companies in which specialist expertise is exchanged and enriches work. It is not based solely on the idea of eliminating work duplication.

Our interview confirmed that the dominant challenge facing management is addressing the cultural divide separating the two national banks. External perceptions in Finland of a 'take-over by the big Swedish brother' and in both markets of the need to convince both employees and clients of the virtues of the merger have created, in our view, a serious challenge for the management team. A number of challenges remain for the future: the creation of an integrated retail banking platform, the possible integration of Norwegian and Danish banks into the proposed Nordic model, and the universal problem of generating revenue growth in a relatively stagnant marketplace. In both Finland and Sweden, their competitors note very little evidence of operational integration. We sense that meeting investor expectations from the merger is placing the management team under heavy stress.

Yet in the two years since the merger, a great deal of progress has been made. The management team has held together under the strong leadership of Hans Dalborg, a satisfactory ROE of 16 per cent was achieved in 1998, and progress has been made in solving several of the problems of the predecessor banks, such as Merita's massive book of real estate investments. And an agreed bid was made in 1999 for Christiania Bank in Norway which may be approved by the Norwegian Government as major stockholder.

On balance, we draw several conclusions from this case study. First, cross-border mergers are just as difficult to execute as most bankers believe! An enormous management effort has been made in selling the merger internally and externally – in addition to running the existing businesses in very competitive markets. Second, it is difficult to see much stockholder value being added in the intermediate term from the merger. Such value will presumably be delivered in the longer term, when MeritaNordbanken as an early mover in Nordic consolidation hopefully can gain a competitive edge over rivals who remained focused on their national market or, like Handelsbanken, expanded organically in the Nordic region. As so often the case, investors will decide whether the long-term advantages offset the current costs of integration.

Bank Mergers

CHASE MANHATTAN: INCLUSIVE MERGERS CREATE DEMONSTRABLE STOCKHOLDER VALUE

The accolades of praise from every side – competitors, consultants and investors – directed at Chase Manhattan's management team for its pair of mergers since 1991 are overwhelming – and, given the volatility of market opinion, possibly frightening. What was a group of three struggling New York money centre banks in 1991 has become a paragon of business focus, stockholder value orientation, an inclusive, 'win–win' culture, and bottom-line results that cannot be denied.

With particular reference to its wholesale business, Figure 11.1 summarises why these various constituencies are so liberal with their praise.

The Chase team has attained leadership positions in a variety of profitable market segments. With a balance between domestic and international as well as consumer vs. corporate banking, Chase has more diversification than most peers. Management has allocated its capital with admirable discipline. The bank has shown impressive growth in market-related income, yet it has not suffered as much as its competitors from the volatility of recent years. Two cost-cutting mergers have each slashed the combined cost base by 18–19 per cent without client service or internal morale having suffered unduly. And ROE of 18 per cent in 1998 is among the best in its peer group.

Figure 11.1   Chase: a proxy for wholesale restructuring

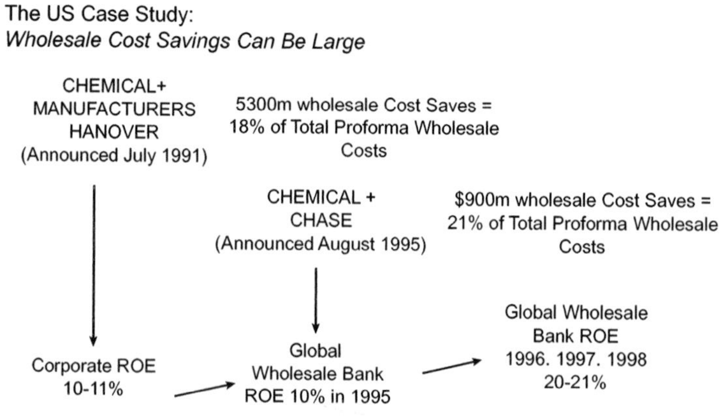

The US Case Study:
Wholesale Cost Savings Can Be Large

CHEMICAL+
MANUFACTURERS
HANOVER
(Announced July 1991)

5300m wholesale Cost Saves =
18% of Total Proforma Wholesale
Costs

CHEMICAL +
CHASE
(Announced August 1995)

$900m wholesale Cost Saves =
21% of Total Proforma Wholesale
Costs

Corporate ROE
10-11%

Global
Wholesale Bank
ROE 10% in 1995

Global Wholesale
Bank ROE
1996. 1997. 1998
20-21%

Source: Goldman Sachs and company documents.

Walter Shipley's management team attributes the success of these two mergers of equals to values which are absent in many contemporary mergers – particularly in the US. Co-opting the senior executives of partner banks in a top management team without playing the ego game is a refreshing sight in a business which often appears to be dominated by personal agendas. Chase's MOM (Merger Oversight Model) is a remarkably detailed framework for merger integration, yet it seems to have been applied sensibly. Communicating values such as trust and co-operation fits the paradigm recommended by the consultant fraternity, who applaud the commitment to building professional skills rather than simply take over a merger partner. The phrase 'it's our merger, not the client's' highlights a weakness of many other mergers. And emphasising that the merged entity is a totally new bank with new possibilities seems to have helped to retain and build a unique skills base.

The key lesson from not just one but two successful mergers is that a strong leadership team can indeed blend financial discipline with attractive values. As the Chase people themselves will be quick to admit, theirs are not perfect mergers, but the end result seems to satisfy all the relevant constituencies. A second lesson is the central importance of leadership in achieving this outstanding result – and a leadership committed to inclusion rather than dominance of a single individual or team.

UBS: SOME 'BUMPS ON THE ROAD' FROM A MERGER MADE IN HEAVEN

The merger announced in late 1997 of two of the largest Swiss banks had all the ingredients of a successful merger. A clearly dominant team from SBC with a track record of successfully blending and shaping different cultures in a meritocratic environment; the creation of a more credible global investment bank to meet the challenge of the US leaders as well as a more viable Swiss retail banking network; the biggest global competitor in the coveted wealth management business, and projected cost savings of 22 per cent which rivalled the best achieved even in the US market. Merger planning moved ahead swiftly, with the top 300 jobs filled within one month from the date of merger announcement.

Several unexpected 'bumps on the road', however, have dented both management's reputation for merger skills as well as its bottom-line profits. One of the reasons for undertaking the merger was the former UBS's perceived lack of control of its market risk positions, a subject dear to the heart of SBC's top team and one which the bank felt totally comfortable in addressing. When market volatility soared in 1998, however, the bank took losses of SF 1.6 billion in exposure to Long Term Capital Management (LTCM) and the former UBS global derivatives book not identified by the SBC team in its due diligence. Earnings for the first merger year thus fell far short of the trajectory planned for the merger period.

The resulting embarrassment led to the departure of the merged bank's chairman, who had helped shaped the merger and championed the interests of his former colleagues from the old UBS. Combined with less than total sensitivity in handling the integration of investment banking professionals from the old UBS, this led to a mass exodus which only benefited the group's competitors. Even a number of former SBC executives in the original management board were shifted in subsequent realignments.

The strengths of the merged group will in all likelihood ensure that it will achieve its long-term strategic goals as well as the substantial projected cost savings, which seem to be well in hand. The investment banking and Swiss retail conversions were achieved within their planned time frame, and other dimensions of the merger process are on track. Yet the main lesson of the UBS merger is that even merger-toughened management teams playing very strong hands can stumble on issues where they can deservedly claim to be experienced. And when they do, and it impacts the bottom line seriously, the financial markets can react without mercy.

HYPOVEREINSBANK: INHERITED LOSSES SPLIT 'MERGER OF THE BEST'

Another European bank merger, that of the two leading Bavarian regional banks, also set off with justifiable high hopes. Although neither bank had mega-merger experience, the union created Germany's second largest bank with an impressive 12 per cent share of the lucrative home mortgage market and attractive portions of other segments such as fund management. Most interesting of all in the inflexible German labour market, the merger promised substantial cost savings of 14 per cent of the combined cost base.

An extended merger period of up to five years – driven in part by the need to wait almost a year for the necessary approvals – was a negative, as well as the significant cultural differences between the conservative Vereinsbank culture and the more adventurous one at HypoBank. On the other hand, management committed itself to a meritocratic selection process and an important repositioning of the bank to maximise stockholder value.

Within a month of the closing of the merger in 1998, however, management revealed the need to provision an extra DM 3.5 billion for the former Hypo Bank's real estate portfolio. This action split the management down the middle along the divide between the two merging entities, which first delayed the naming of the management team and finally, two years later provoked the departure of seven of the senior ex-Hypo management, including all Hypo members of the Management Board. Subsequent unanticipated real estate provisions – perhaps from the Hypo portfolio as well – depressed current earnings for 1999 and helped contribute to a 50 per cent fall in the stock price from the 1998 high.

While the merger is on target in terms of cost saves, the management faces continued internal conflict between embittered factions blaming each other for past mistakes as well as the need to struggle to achieve bottom-line earnings targets.

One lesson from this case study is the limited value of due diligence, even when, as management points out, Hypo Bank was known to have had additional potential loss exposure in real estate loans and auditors were specifically asked to validate its quality. Whether management ignored the resulting findings or whether they were used as a weapon to oust Hypo Bank executives, the end result has been a serious internal conflict which must have a long-term negative impact. Secondly, HVB is a classic case study of how such an incident can aggravate an existing cultural difference between two merging banks with dramatic consequences for stockholder value. Unlike the case of First Union in the US, however, the resulting depressed stock price has not undermined the planned expansion strategy of a 'bank of the regions'.

FORTIS: AN OPPORTUNISTIC ACQUISITION STRATEGY LEADS TO A MORE FOCUSED INSTITUTION

One of the new breed of cross-border *bancassurance* mergers formed in the 'Class of 1990', Fortis started life essentially as an insurance group with a banking appendage. By 1999, with the acquisition of Générale Bank, it had become largely a banking institution with a much smaller insurance component. An equally significant change in 1999 was the decision to move from a geographic structure built around relatively autonomous operating units to a more integrated business run on functional lines.

During the 1990s Fortis management aggressively – and opportunistically – bid for a number of commercial banks, private banking institutions and insurers in its core Benelux market. In the case of Générale Bank, it bid despite the open opposition of a group of executive directors of the bank. It now is by far the largest Belgian bank with 30 per cent of the market and also holds a 21 per cent share of the Benelux fund management sector.

As the decade drew to a close, however, the decision was made to integrate the businesses. The 'super brand' Fortis is replacing centuries-old names such as Générale Bank, the banking and insurance businesses will be run as functional entities, and cost savings will be squeezed – probably painfully – out of the Belgian bank merger. Contributing factors include the prospect of improved revenues from applying ASLK's skills in selling insurance products to other banks in the group as well as the opportunities for cost reduction in Générale Bank.

A major lesson from this case study in our view is the pressure exerted by market forces on a former loose association of banks and insurers to improve financial results by greater integration. Having paid a generous price in the battle for Générale Bank, Fortis like its American peers needs to recoup additional earnings to justify the price paid.

As a friend in Fortis admits, referring to the integration of Générale Bank and the projected reduction of about 5,000 jobs in that market:

It's not all sunshine! We've realised that banking and insurance professionals have hung on to their old concepts, but the customer couldn't care less about these traditions!

The managerial challenge is a real one, as the same cross-cultural issues (between Belgian and Dutch as well as insurance and banking executives) exist as in the MeritaNordbanken merger. The tensions inherent in the integration process will, in our view, aggravate these differences as Fortis attempts to maximise stockholder value.

LLOYDS TSB: DISCIPLINE IN MERGER SELECTION AND EXECUTION

Lloyds TSB won our straw poll for success in European mergers just as it has won accolades from investors and peer banks for its commitment to stockholder value, superior ROE and lean cost/income ratio. As we have seen in earlier chapters, management attributes this success to its financial disciplines in rigorously evaluating investment opportunities and pursuing a course of action which will maximise stockholder value towards previously defined targets. Of all the banks in our universe, Lloyds TSB is the only one prepared to commit itself to a stockholder value target measured in terms of stockholder value increase (defined as total stockholder return–stock price appreciation plus dividend): a doubling every three years, a target it has achieved for some 15 years.

In a merger context, this means fixing a price – for both acquisitions and divestitures – which is realistic in terms of alternative uses of funds as well as the gains to be made from a sale or purchase. Such discipline is combined with imagination and innovation: Lloyds historically has been an early mover in *bancassurance*, acquiring a building society, bidding for other large UK commercial banks such as Standard Chartered and Midland. The end result – a price book value of five times and ROE exceeding 30 per cent – is the envy of peers across the world.

In the case of the TSB acquisition, Lloyds was driven by the strategic goal of reducing its combined cost/income ratio, which at 43 per cent in 1999 is by far the lowest of the major full line UK commercial banks. It has achieved the 11 per cent combined cost reduction projected for the merger, and at the same time built its skills base by retaining many of the senior management of its acquisition.

For our purposes, the lesson of its merger experience is that a cost reduction strategy can be successfully pursued by a disciplined approach to pricing and execution without some of the excesses seen in the US. At the same time, an inclusive approach to the merger has borne fruit. Lloyds has not made expensive purchases in popular businesses such as fund management and investment banking. Its challenge for the future, however, is to continue to implement its strategy and maintain its return on investor funds without suffering the dilution implied by the cross-border mergers contemplated by so many of its European peers. The market believes that Lloyds TSB would prefer to return capital to its stockholders rather than suffer such dilution, thus respecting their governing objective of maximising stockholder value and not growth for its own sake.

WELLS FARGO: A NEW US MEGA-MERGER MODEL EMERGES

By successfully initiating its merger of equals with the former Wells Fargo, the management of Norwest not only doubled its physical size but also undertook a management transformation requiring the blending of two sharply different cultures. The new bank now has retail strength in the American West and Mid-West with nation-wide distribution of key products such as direct lending to small businesses and mortgage origination. Previous mergers undertaken by the Norwest team involved much smaller entities.

One of the challenges facing management is typified by the example of failed integration of First Interstate by the old Wells, which attempted too much too fast in its systems conversion: migrating concurrently two major conversion projects, an exodus of experienced staff in the acquired bank which opted for generous severance packages, and too short a timetable for the overall exercise. The result – a 12 per cent deposit loss – wrecked the merger economics.

Arguably an even more serious challenge for the future is the cultural one: the old Wells was known and respected for its 'high tech' strategy involving low-cost alternative distribution channels and the maximum use of technology. In contrast, Norwest had won widespread acclaim for its 'high touch' approach to client relationships involving a complex mix of relationship management skills, management information and a focus on revenue maximisation.

In a conscious effort to build a totally new bank leveraging the strength of each culture – as well as build a new retail IT platform – Wells Fargo management has emphasised agreement on values and merger process over short-term financial results in the form of a relatively long three-year merger period and fairly modest cost gains of 8 per cent of the combined base. Such an inclusive approach is reminiscent of the Chase Manhattan philosophy – but without the substantial cost savings.

To date the market seems to have welcomed this potential new merger model by according Wells premium valuation parameters. The issue raised by the merger is whether the cultural challenge can be successfully addressed and the financial targets achieved. If this is the case and the result is welcomed by the financial markets, there could well be less pressure on US merger candidates in the future to risk dislocation by driving for massive short-term financial results.

FIRST UNION: A RARE STUMBLE BUT A BIG ONE

Having acquired over 75 banks since 1985 and built a solid reputation as a successful 'serial acquirer', First Union suffered well-publicised problems in the integration of its largest purchase, the \$17 billion acquisition of Core States in Philadelphia in 1998. The resulting revenue loss has thus dented both First Union's 1998–99 earnings as well as its stock price, which at one point fell by one-third following the news of the Core States problem.

The strategic value of Core States was clear: acquiring Philadelphia's largest bank would give First Union, which already owned a bank in nearby New Jersey, a leading market share in the US Mid-Atlantic region to complement its strength in the South East. Core States' clients could then be converted to the new Future Bank platform in which First Union had invested an estimated \$300 million. To do so, however, meant paying a record price of over five times book. Chairman Ed Crutchfield at the time was quoted as saying:

> When you're in an industry that is consolidating, the time to do a transaction of this kind is when you can.[1]

But to achieve the savings needed to justify this price, First Union had to accelerate the conversion process as well as deal with major cultural differences. A contemporary newspaper account contrasted Core States' 'touchy-feely culture with First Union's Darwinian style of management'.[2]

As we have seen in Chapter 3, First Union decided to proceed with a twelve-month conversion period and cost reduction of 40 per cent of Core States' cost base at the same time as the combined group was converting the entire organisation to its new Future Bank retail platform. In addition, the bank had to segment out clients accounts being transferred to other banks and execute a multiple conversion because of Core States' uncompleted earlier merger with Meridian Bank.

The result was an estimated double-digit loss of customers and revenues during the merger year 1998 and the need to supplement staff shortages in Core States with additional employees. The negative publicity and impact on the stock price was substantial, and the Core States problem contributed to several earnings warnings by First Union during 1999.

While the customer losses in Philadelphia have largely been made good and the conversion completed, the lesson from this episode – as well as the similar problems encountered earlier by Wells with its First Interstate merger – has been an important one. Not only can an experienced merger practitioner stumble seriously by over-committing on a single transaction, but also its reputation and stock price can be impaired for a much longer period of time. The latter means that an aggressive acquisition strategy can be sidelined while competitors move ahead with their deals.

12 How Banks See the Future

Our last question to each of our interviewees was their view of the future merger prospects. What had they learned from their own merger experience that might drive their own future behaviour? How did they view the merger strategies of their peers and competitors? And perhaps most important of all, had banks learned from their merger experience, and how might that experience drive future merger behaviour?

THE CONSENSUS VIEW

The overwhelming response was that current merger trends would continue – if not accelerate and intensify. We had anticipated a greater number of dissenters from the view expressed daily in the financial press as the old millennium drew to a close, but it was not to be. The image of an unstoppable locomotive on its way to an endgame destination is on the minds of the great majority of our senior bankers. Three quotations typify the dominant view in Europe:

Bernard Michel of Credit Agricole:

> The merger wave will continue in Europe. In-market deals will lead to strategic alliances [similar to theirs with Banca Intesa in Italy] with foreign banks. We'll have a European market; Europe is being created. There's lots of capital looking to be invested which needs more than a money market return. People will diversify out of their core business into areas like consumer finance and custody. We'll have two or three major banks in each country, and banks will develop central processing units for separate distribution channels. Cost cutting, the desire to protect oneself, and the need to invest in technology for the Internet and other projects will all drive more mergers.

Juergen Krumnow, former *Vorstand* member of Deutsche Bank:

> It's now become clear that the best way forward in Europe is a national merger. You should try to create value at home and then look abroad. It's essential to have a big market share at home.

Pedro Libano Monteiro of BCP:

> There will be more concentration. It's like the oil business: you need
> to be bigger and more efficient. It's not just the US model of cutting
> costs by closing branches, but of offering more services to clients off
> the same expense base. The first priority is in-market deals with
> cross-border transactions coming later. The cultural dimension for
> these latter is a wholly different thing. Look at Portugal and Spain:
> we're right next door to each other but have had over 800 years of
> separate development. So such deals will take place after the in-
> market ones. Market capitalisation is critical for our survival. The
> BPA transaction was essential for us; even now with over $5 billion
> of market cap we're still an easy target.

The cultural issue inherent in cross-border European mergers is top
of mind for many senior bankers as they contemplate with which
foreign culture they would be most comfortable. As Wilco ten Berg
of ABN Amro, which has given the contemplation of cross-border
deals a high priority, explains:

> We all want to get bigger and prefer in-market deals to do so. But we
> also have to think of which culture outside the Netherlands we can
> work best with in a merger of equals.

In this context, regionalism is very much on the minds of European
bankers. Andreas Treichl of Erste Bank expresses a common view:

> Mergers have become part of our life, as the number of senior
> managers with merger experience is increasing. In the US, where
> mergers are easier to execute than here, the weight of US banks
> globally will increase as this trend continues. In our endgame in
> Europe, I see about four or five major banks in each region. For us
> the logical region is Central and Eastern Europe [the CEE], which
> includes Austria as well as former communist countries such as the
> Czech Republic and Hungary. If the CEE develops quickly, we can
> become one of these four to five banks in the region. If not, we'll
> have to become part of another region!

Regionalism preoccupies the minds of bankers at the other ends of
Europe. Soren Andersson of Swedbank speaks of the 'Nordicum',
which includes the Baltic countries as well as the Nordic region, Poland

and North Germany and is their own geographic focus. Following the announcement of BBV's merger with Argentaria, Emilio Ybarra of BBV refers to his vision of a 'grand Latin bank' with strategic alliances in Italy, France and Portugal.

As the European merger wave rolls on, a few voices are raised to acknowledge the tensions between the market's demands and the reality of the management challenge. Stefan Ermisch of HVB portrays the dilemma:

> There will be more deals, and we have learned a lot – both positive and negative – about how to do them. The markets are forcing the pace, and not all the mergers will be successful. We started early in the game; if you succeed in an in-market merger you'll be better prepared for the cross-border ones. But will the market support this process? We have to deliver on our targets. But we're not obliged to go further; we could stop at the first deal.

One of his former HVB colleagues speaks his mind on the same topic:

> Lots of bank mergers don't work, but there's an unstoppable trend towards huge conglomerates. What is the 'market'? It's the fund managers, the investment bankers, the traders and research people, each of which makes a ton of money with each deal. Bankers are stupid enough to believe all this about cost synergies, but even if you follow their advice you'll be a target in a few years. Will the new business model of the Internet change all this?

In the US, the cost-driven retail model continues to preoccupy the minds of successful acquirers. Fleet Boston's Brian Moynihan foresees a continuation of the merger trend with the strategic goal of slashing the expense base. Chase Manhattan's Walter Shipley, with a foot in both the corporate and retail banking sectors, predicts a different scenario for each:

> Corporate and investment banking has changed dramatically; lots of players have left the business. The need for global distribution will create about six to eight global investment banks, including Chase and Citigroup from the US. In the consumer business, IT will dramatically change the game. We've had a love/hate relationship with the bank branch. We feel even more strongly today the threats to the traditional broker and bank branch. Our planning

assumption for the next five to ten years is a totally new system which can dramatically reduce our cost base.

At Deutsche Bank, Scott Moeller sees the globalisation trend as the unstoppable locomotive:

> The future will be difficult if you're a regulator. Oligopolies exist in any national banking market, but they'll be even more powerful on a global basis in investment banking. There will be lots more cross-border acquisitions as a result.

WHAT CAN STOP OR SLOW THE SPEEDING LOCOMOTIVE?

What can derail the unstoppable locomotive? The only development mentioned by a large minority of our interviewees is the Internet and e-commerce. Does it make sense to pay a substantial multiple of book value to acquire a retail customer base which tomorrow will either leave you for someone else's Internet facility or will become unprofitable because of Internet pricing? Roberto Nicastro of UniCredito expresses a common concern:

> It's a very complex decision. Should you pay for branches if the competition can cherry-pick your clients off the Internet? It's a growing concern, but it's also clear that you have to pay a premium in Italy even if the book value is not there! The issue is whether paying €1000–2000 per client really increases the value of our bank.

Austin Adams at First Union is more negative:

> I can't imagine the market returning to the 1997 model of paying five times book value. It's unrealistic. The model has changed because of e-commerce and the resulting lower value of a geographic footprint. We're all paying more attention to the value of revenue synergies and watching the Citigroup experience with cross-selling. The issue is how well you can distribute information in the system and break down silos. There's a lot of scepticism about the Citigroup experiment, and analysts will have to dig more deeply into the banking organisation to see how well customer information is shared within the bank.

Phil Ryan of Credit Suisse also reflects a balanced judgement:

> The market loves deals with a value opportunity – not big mergers
> of equals with a cultural quagmine. There's no guaranteed stock
> price increase. There's no evidence that size and scope create
> value. What does is a well-run company with a strong culture.
> In an e-commerce world, size/scope acquisitions could fall apart
> as scale will be a negative against a more flexible and focused
> interloper.

One of the most thoughtful responses to these questions comes from
Rudi Bogni of UBS:

> There are three underlying issues which will determine whether the
> current merger mania will continue. First is the landscape of the
> client base. Globalisation in the sense of providing a global
> service has forced mergers; will it continue? Second is the cost of
> capital as driven by the conglomerate discount. This goes in cycles.
> Today size and scope are king. But tomorrow the market may
> decide it wants specialists and not conglomerates. Thirdly is
> economies of scale. In private banking, for example, the front end
> (client facing) cost is linear: you may even have diseconomies of
> scale. But the process behind it is subject to economies of scale.
> The same for investment banking, for example, in leveraging the
> research function.

Discipline in mergers is an issue for several senior bankers in our
sample – essentially those who regard themselves as disciplined
acquirers in a market populated by rivals anxious to do a deal at any
price. Lloyds TSB, which prides itself on its ability to back away from a
deal if the price is not right, is one of these disciplinarians. Kent
Atkinson expresses his views:

> Most deals in the future will not create much stockholder value.
> We're trying to improve our efficiency through mergers, as opposed
> to geographic expansion in the US and cross-border mergers in
> Europe. In the early 1990s we had big margins in the UK. We said
> to ourselves 'this can't be sustained; we'll have more competitors'.
> We projected what would happen if our margins came down to that
> of the lowest in any country. It showed a net revenue loss for us of
> pounds 1 billion. Oh hell, we said. We can't cut costs that much on

our own – we're already pretty efficient – but with a major in-market acquisition (which turned out to be TSB) we might do something significant. The rest, as they say, is history. But going forward there aren't so many in-market opportunities, and focus is turning to cross-border mergers. I believe the next few years will be characterised by revenue-enhancing cross-border deals. Whereas the 1990s were marked by in-market cost-reduction mergers!

Wells Fargo's Dick Kovacevich is widely viewed as having created a new bank merger model which diverges sharply from the traditional US cost reduction paradigm. He and Walter Shipley are at one in their commitment to values and the creation of a totally new institution through the merger process. Kovacevich also defies conventional Wall Street thinking:

Don't listen to Wall Street. They told me to pay more for smaller acquisitions than do a merger of equals with Wells Fargo. For this deal, they said to cut costs more and merge the systems quickly. They also said the cultures were incompatible. They were wrong, wrong, wrong! Can Wall Street run a bank? You've got to do what's right – what you and your team think is best. You'll always have some merger problems. This isn't an easy job. People who don't learn from their merger mistakes won't be around for long. You have to understand that you don't get better by being bigger. Skills are the key. It's not about economies of scale but of economies of skill – that will build you scale! Big is not better but worse. It's tough to change, to merge systems.

Only a few of our sources expressed concern about their ability to manage the growing size and complexity of merged banks. One of these is Henjo Hielkema of Fortis:

The biggest deterrent to mergers is internal complexity, which is inevitable with larger size. Every three or four years you should reinvent yourself to simplify things – to make yourself understandable again. Mergers keep adding things to the carcass. We did go through such a metamorphosis in 1998 when our structure was dwarfed by the Générale Bank merger.

Den Danske Bank's Leonhardt Pihl articulates a different concern about mergers in the future:

The traditional merger – simply putting banks together – won't be the case in the future. We'll have to be more intelligent. All the banks in the Nordic region look alike in strategy, operations and structure. Management has been dealt a hand of cards and each will have to manage that hand. Driven by shareholder value, we may have to take out businesses and combine them with similar businesses of other banks. That could create new and different management challenges – perhaps more complex than those faced in past mergers.

His fellow Dane, Thorleif Krarup of Unibank, also foresees future problems:

There will be much more consolidation. Our lesson from mergers is to make hard decisions fast but take more time to build a new set of values. Bankers are better at hard decisions but not so good at motivating middle management. It's one of the big future challenges for bank management.

Mergers in the world of investment banking should remain infinitely more difficult than their retail counterparts. The problems encountered by ING's Barings integration and the difficult SBC/UBS merger highlight the challenge of bringing together in a single organisation the highly motivated and individualistic 'masters of the universe'. Citigroup, for example, has not yet attempted to select a single relationship officer from the merged Salomon Smith Barney and Citicorp corporate and investment banking teams – despite the well-known preference for corporate CFOs to deal with a single relationship manager from each provider. This may be one of the tough choices cited by Jack Morris of Citigroup in his comment that:

There is no magic wand for conflict avoidance. There are too many babies that would have to be sliced.

Scott Moeller, a career investment banker charged with co-ordinating the integration of Bankers Trust in Europe into Deutsche Bank's global banking unit, finds it difficult to identify many successful true mergers in the sector:

Merging investment banks together has a lousy history. Most of them involved retaining their identity, like Morgan Stanley and Dean Witter. At Deutsche Bank we decided to merge immediately to prevent the development of a separate BT identity within Deutsche Bank.

Faced with the likelihood of more mergers – including, in Europe, the cross-border variety – management has been thinking deeply about the value of their culture and the damage that might be done by a large merger of equals. We discussed above the reaction, for example, of ABN Amro. The dumbbell theory propagated by many management consultants – a handful of very big banks balanced by a number of much smaller specialists with little in between – is accepted by most if not all bankers. But in practice the banking world is full of mid-sized banks which have thrived without undertaking massive mergers. In our universe, such mid-sized groups like DnB, Handelsbanken and BCP would seem to prefer to eschew mega-mergers rather than risk compromising their culture and the competitive strength it provides.

Given the virtual unanimity of our universe's vision for the future, the obvious issue to be addressed in our concluding chapter is whether it is a sound one. What, if anything, could derail the speeding locomotive of consolidation? What shape might such consolidation take?

13 Our Own View: Some Guidelines for the Future

The views of our interviewees from the preceding chapters are clear. By and large our senior bankers agree with the consulting fraternity on the key dimensions of merger execution, and they are certainly in accord among themselves on how the banking sector will evolve in the future. There are discordant notes struck on the trade-off between speed of execution and the arguments for a more leisurely pace, as well as a few worries about the Internet and how to manage tomorrow's larger and more complex institutions, but by and large a strong consensus exists on most key issues.

So what can we add to this consensus? We listed in the earlier chapters a number of issues which seemed worthy of debate. Some have been addressed in subsequent chapters, and in this concluding one we shall opine on the remainder. Most of the latter relate either to the likely ability to achieve stated goals or the best means of achieving them. In sum, is the consensus on future behaviour a durable one? Are there inherent inconsistencies or disequilibria in its various assumptions? How about external forces such as the Internet? Will 'the market' continue to support the consensus?

It might be useful to start with some reflections on the key issues raised in earlier chapters.

BLENDING PEOPLE AND CULTURES

Our first observation is the almost overwhelming challenge in human terms of blending massive and complex banking institutions. Whether termed 'cultural change' or 'people problems', it is inherent in all of the transactions profiled in this book. We have seen how European banks in the early 1990s underestimated cultural differences, while even the most skilled US serial acquirers at the end of the decade drastically misjudged the human dimension of integrating both customers and professional staff. The analogy that strikes us is that of declaring war: the protagonists may have a good sense of objectives and strategy, but in the smoke of the battlefield a totally unexpected outcome may result.

121

One can argue – and we do so below – that certain cultures and leadership styles are more or less well equipped to deal with transformational change, but the challenge is a daunting one for all. Consider the multitude of dilemmas faced by merger leadership:

First is the conflict between speed and such parameters as fairness and equality, building trust, preserving the virtues of local character, and meritocracy. Speed of execution maximises savings and enhances clarity, but it runs directly counter to the need to familiarise the partners with each other and to build common cultural values. The use of co-CEOs and co-department heads, for example, improves mutual understanding but at the expense of speed and clarity of decision-making. Professor Philippe Haspeslagh of INSEAD articulates the ideal:

> In practice the key is to find the right balance between speed in the formal integration and progress in the merging of minds.[1]

Second is the battle between size/scope and flexibility/responsiveness. We discuss below the merits and demerits of size from a strategic standpoint, but in management terms today's large and complex organisations rarely have the ability to respond flexibly and effectively to the needs of either client segments or professional units. Discipline can be a laudable management value, but applying its dictates to the likes of fund managers and investment bankers is not a simple task.

Third is the infinitely complex process of people and systems selection in a mega-merger. To varying degrees, the banks in our universe strive for some form of meritocratic or fair selection process, but overshadowing this effort is the perceived need for speed and, in many cases, the suspicion that the dominant partner will ultimately make the key decisions to favour its personnel and systems. Equality of representation on management boards, co-CEOs and heads of departments and equality of economic interests of the respective stockholders are common solutions to this dilemma, but each can be opposed by valid arguments to the contrary.

Lastly, the time frame for cultural change is a multiple of that of the merger period. As so many of our senior bankers point out, when confronted with massive change, the natural human response is to resist change and look to the good old days of the old bank, despite the blandishments of the 'new bank' – especially if it requires demanding performance standards! Some thoughtful CEOs like Dick Kovacevich and Thorleif Krarup acknowledge this gap in plotting their own strategies, but most of their peers feel obliged to drive massive change over a two–three-year period on the basis of arguments for their brave new world and the need to achieve performance targets for survival.

A related dimension is that of the 'friendly' as opposed to 'unfriendly' merger. Our analysis forces us to look beyond the headlines and more deeply into the personal agendas of the key individuals affected. In our view each professional will decide for him or herself whether the transaction is friendly or not. And even the friendliest of deals usually requires a significant behavioural change.

THE NEED FOR SUPERIOR LEADERSHIP SKILLS

These challenges are inherent in the merger environment, and for a variety of reasons the merger process will continue in one form or another in banking as well as a host of other business. This leads to *our second observation, which is the need for superlative leadership skills to master the challenge of comprehensive change.* Here the issue is not the need, but the availability of the requisite talents.

As in our research for *Leadership in Financial Institutions*[2] our conclusions are mixed. One particular quotation from Bill Crozier, a former US bank CEO known for his own leadership skills, strikes home:

> You need a vision to make it work – a clear view of what the goal is. This is not a democracy – I'd prefer a tyrant who knows what he's doing! The industry doesn't have a lot of strong people. There are some very bright guys but not a lot of vision, and often the brainwaves aren't there. As Morris Schapiro, the eminent bank stock dealer often put it, 'there are more banks than bankers'.

In our universe, there are clearly leaders of vision with a strong track record in the merger business. Walter Shipley, Dick Kovacevich, Sir Brian Pitman of Lloyds TSB, Jorge Gonçalves of BCP and Angel Corcostegui of BSCH are among those in our universe which come to mind. In addition, the leadership of a number of US serial acquirers have proven their ability to create a merger machine which absorbs acquisitions with reasonable efficiency.

Yet in many other institutions the leadership is split in a collective group such as a Dutch or German Management Board with collective responsibility or a Japanese bank where former CEOs share effective responsibility. In others, the CEO may be a competent and experienced senior banker but faced with his first major merger challenge.

The bottom line for us on this issue is that successful mergers in the future require ultimately one of those unique individuals who successfully blend determination and vision, unique people skills and empathy, and the energy to spend 25 hours a day communicating the message as well as running the bank. A collective entity can also do the job, but success requires a unique level of common purpose within that entity – or else a leader who can exercise effective power in that small group. Whatever the leadership structure, all the evidence points to the need for extraordinary communication skills, the ability to project physically one's personality to literally thousands of colleagues, and an untiring commitment to the communication process.

The pressures on the limited number of qualified CEOs are intense. And the abrupt departures in 1999 alone of such senior executives from First Union, Bank One, Kapital Holding and Swedbank within our universe confirm that the top job in bank mergers today is no sinecure.

INFORMATION TECHNOLOGY (IT) AS A LITMUS TEST FOR SUCCESSFUL MERGER EXECUTION

The ubiquitous issue of IT selection and integration should be viewed in this context of conflict and stress. There is a remarkably strong consensus among our interviewees, both consultants and bankers, on the appropriate process for addressing these questions. The technical choice and conversion process may be complex, but the greater problem, at least in Europe, has been the decision-making process. Thus the desire to please a number of constituencies and to select the 'best of the best' systems has often both extended the merger period and produced a higher cost solution.

The experience of Bernard Michel of Credit Agricole must have been duplicated across many in our universe as they struggled with IT decisions. Choice of systems means jobs and prestige as well as functionality and cost, and arguments may well be driven by the understandable human desire to protect such jobs and images.

Thus the cost and timing of a major IT decision is often a litmus-paper test of successful merger execution. Strong leadership from the top, experience in previous mergers, the ability to stick to a demanding time frame, and willingness to make efficient trade-offs between functionality and cost are all vital elements. Going forward, IT decisions may be facilitated by the introduction of common architecture as well as outsourcing and package solutions, but we suspect that the managerial challenges will remain.

As for converting the merged bank to a new system, experience helps, but the examples of First Union and Wells Fargo show that practice does not necessarily make perfect! As long as bank leadership demands substantial and early cost saves, the conversion risk will remain.

INTEGRATION VS. FEDERATION: IS THERE AN IDEAL STRUCTURE?

One of the few issues which separates our merger universe is that of management structure. The US model of a single CEO and fully integrated, line-of-business operating structures contrasts sharply with the collective management/co-head leadership and a decentralised federal approach of many European – and probably, in the future – Japanese banks.

The merits and demerits of each are well known and vigorously articulated by their advocates. There is certainly no single answer, but several points should be made. First, there is a decided trend even in Europe away from the federal model which is driven largely by the need to improve profit performance. Thus in recent years Fortis, Argentaria and the former Santander have moved to integrate part or all of their federated businesses, while UniCredito has also moved toward the BCP model of a single IT platform but multiple client-facing brands. Whether they move as far as Bank One with a single brand is a separate issue, but the centralised processing model has clear attractions. The issue for many others, such as ING, MeritaNordbanken and Dexia, is when to make the hefty and possibly divisive investment in common facilities so as to reduce the costly spend on multiple systems. In many respects, the choice is between pain today and pain tomorrow, and it is not an easy one.

By the same token, the outlook for multiple leadership is unclear. For many institutions, the use of co-CEOs and heads of function is a temporary solution, as in the case of Citigroup, for a portion of the merger period. The *Vorstand* model will probably survive, but it is being undermined in some businesses like fund management and investment banking which do not lend themselves to collective decision-making.

WHICH IS BEST: COST-CUTTING OR REVENUE-GENERATING MERGERS?

For many of our interviewees, the battle-lines have been drawn between advocates of cost saving and revenue-generating mergers. In our view, there is room for both, perhaps in the same merger transaction. Banks have a strategic need to reduce their cost base, but their need for revenue growth is arguably equally dire. While generating a dollar of extra revenue may be more difficult than cutting costs by an equal amount, that extra revenue for a bank with a 50 per cent cost/income ratio is worth twice the cost saving. The classic US cost-cutting model can clearly be an efficient machine, yet it has its limitations in stimulating revenue growth and cross-selling. The success of the Wells Fargo and Fleet/Bank of Boston transactions, for different reasons, will therefore be watched with interest.

Certainly the rarer of the breed will be the revenue-generating genus, given the need to generate a culture of openness and the management systems required for successful execution. Here the BCP/BPA and Wells Fargo mergers are the transactions to study.

We agree that a strategy based solely on cost saving deals may not meet market expectations. Ed Furash, a veteran US banking consultant, is most articulate on this point:

> consultants come to banks with pat re-engineering schemes to reduce costs overnight to peer standards ... the result [has been] a depressed, mourning workforce, diminished customer service, and weakened revenue. It has been impossible for banks to save their way to salvation ... mergers *per se* do not necessarily produce cost savings; management execution does.[3]

THE BARGAIN BETWEEN INVESTORS AND BANK MANAGEMENT

This brings us to the issue of 'the market' and its demands. *Underlying these and so many other merger issues is the Faustian bargain between institutional investors on the one hand and bank management on the other, with the investment banking community actively involved in intermediating the process.* During the 1990s this bargain has been hewn into a finely-crafted contract. Bank managements wish to grow their business, preserve their independence, win accolades for size and other performance benchmarks, raise capital cheaply and acquire other financial institutions on as favourable terms as possible.

Institutional investors, on the other hand, have viewed bank consolidation as the dominant justification for increasing their holdings in an industry which by many standards is a drab commodity business characterised by slow organic growth, overcapacity, lower cost competitors and the ability to lose large amounts of money in a relatively short period of time. The investment banking community has successfully promoted the concept of the dominance of market capitalisation and helped individual banks to make skilful use of it.

The result has been a massive increase in institutional ownership – inevitably Anglo-Saxon in origin – in bank stocks across the developed world. This investment is underpinned by a number of assumptions. One is the importance of size, which we discuss below. Another is the related issue of stockholder value created by mergers, which, as we discussed in Chapter 3, has been translated into the net present value of future cost savings. The final element is the prospect of a finite endgame, in which only a few eligible candidates will theoretically remain for both bank management and investors.

The formula was applied initially in the US, where an almost formulaic relationship between cost saves and market appreciation has evolved. In Europe and Japan, as we have discussed, the formula works less well, but the concept still drives behaviour.

Applying the formula, however, in a market dominated by buyers anxious to be among those remaining standing in the endgame led to a predicable result in the second half of the 1990s. As Figure 13.1 shows, in the US (as well as Europe and Japan) valuation parameters have rocketed. At the same time, the imbalance between supply and demand has transferred virtually all of the value created by the merger to the seller's stockholders. Figure 13.2 portrays data gathered by the Bank for International Settlements to quantify what has come to be known as the 'winners' curse'.

Events at the close of the 1990s, however, may have shaken the faith in the bargain in at least some members of the investment community. We have seen in Figure 10.1 that the bank stock premium over market averages in Europe has suffered since reaching its peak in 1998. Disappointment in failure to achieve merger goals has been vividly demonstrated in the collapse of stock prices for banks like HVB, First Union and Bank One.

Our conversations with bank analysts and consultants confirm that the investment community has become far more discriminating. Bob

Figure 13.1 US bank valuation parameters soar

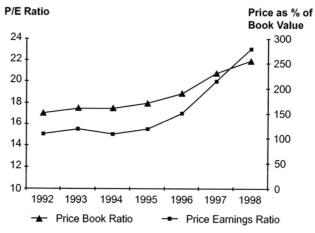

Source: SNL Securities LP.

Figure 13.2 Comparative share price responses to mergers and acquisitions

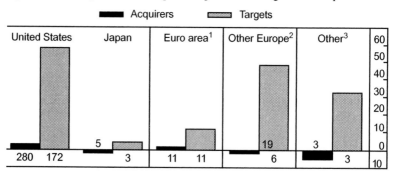

Average returns in excess of the banking sector index over a two-month window centred on the announcement date of the transaction: the figures in the graph indicate the number of cases for which share prices were available during the period January 1994–January 1999. 1 France, Germany, Italy, Spain, Portugal and Finland. 2 Denmark, Sweden, Switzerland and the United Kingdom. 3 Australia and Canada.
Sources: IFR Securities Data; Datastream; BIS.

Yates, a senior and highly respected financial institutions analyst with Fox-Pitt Kelton in London, summarises his perspective:

In the US, there was originally clear value creation. But with prices rising to as much as five times book value, the process has matured.

And Europe plays by different rules. European bank management is not well positioned to create value. There's a lack of transparency and level of political interference in Europe that would be blown away in the US. Investment banks have created expectations; bank management believes that it has to do something with the market values they have been given.

Across the Atlantic, Chip Dickson, a senior US bank analyst with Salomon Smith Barney, also expresses concern:

> The market is saying 'I don't trust you any more.' Discount rates for future merger cost savings are rising from 10 per cent to 20 per cent. The premium paid in the US over book value tripled in 1998, and too much is being given away to selling stockholders. The market looks at the frequent acquirers, and given the number of disappointments has become skeptical.

Dickson makes an effort to adjust for the increased investment – and exposure – by such serial acquirers by calculating the pooling premium – essentially the goodwill above book value – which would have to be written off if the value of the securities offered in a merger were to fall below the value at which they were issued. As Table 13.1 shows, this premium for the major US banks soared to $168 billion at the end of 1998 compared to $257 billion of capital at book value. By his calculations, this pooling premium in 1998 accounted for 23 per cent of the market capitalisation of the major US banks, up from 9 per cent in 1996.

Table 13.1   Growth in value of pooling premium[a] for Salomon Smith Barney bank composite, 1995–1998 (amounts in $ billion)

	1995	1998
(A) Total invested capital on purchase basis[b]	$125	$257
PLUS: cumulative pooling premium[a]	17	169
EQUALS: Total invested capital on pooling basis	142	426
(B) Total market capitalisation	223	729
(C) Pooling premium as % of market capitalisation	7.6%	23.1%

Source: Salomon Smith Barney.
[a] Cumulative difference between value of securities offered on pooling basis and on purchase basis (book value).
[b] Book value of common equity adjusted for intangibles, loss reserve and restructuring charges.

Another respected US bank analyst, Nancy Bush of Ryan Beck, describes her view of the current bargain with investors:

US bank stocks are depressed. Serial acquirers are selling at dismal price/earnings ratios. The distrust of mergers is rational. There's a serious risk that the market has changed direction. Some banks have already been permanently impaired because of their low valuation ratios. They're stuck with what they've got and may just trail off into irrelevance.

Susan Leadem, the highly rated head of Goldman Sachs' London-based bank stock group, emphasises the uncertainty involved in predicting future behaviour:

It's hard to predict success. It's a moving target. Banks get caught up in their style. Bank One believed for years in its model, but the world is changing, and they've gone off to another model. People aren't getting smarter, and market capitalisation still drives it all. You have to learn from your mistakes.

Another experienced sell side analyst, Matt Czepliewicz of Salomon Smith Barney in London, describes the pressures on management emanating from the bargain:

Most European banks have fallen short in delivering what they promised. The market wants quantified and challenging targets, and management is under great pressure to promise synergies and accretion that they themselves know lie at the limit of what is realistic. The shortfalls are in head count and branch reduction, the expense of IT development and conversion – essentially a combination of little things that make mergers work. In 1998 and 1999 the aggressive push to do deals meant that a lot of buyers abandoned their IRR [internal rate of return] hurdle rates. In the early days the buyer could generate a positive IRR, but now the added value has all been handed over to the seller.

Figure 13.3 from a 1999 report by Goldman Sachs shows how sensitive the market has become to recent announcements of European bank deals as measured by the movement in combined market capitalisation during the month following the merger announcement divided by the net present value of the cost saves. Thus the initial market reaction ranged from a positive 443 per cent for the HVB merger to a negative 9 per cent for the Deutsche Bank/Bankers Trust fusion.

Figure 13.3 Wide range of market response to projected cost savings

Cost Savings Announced in
Recent Major Deals

	Cost Savings as a % of Total Cost Base	Market Reaction/ NPV of Cost Savings
UBS/SBC	19%	37%
BCH/Banco Santander'	9%	209%
Hypobank/Vereinsbank	14%	443%
UniCredito/Credito Italiano	4%	115%
Societe Generale/Paribas	14%	0%
Deutsche Bank/Bankers Trust	6%	9%

Note: 1. Cost base excluding Latin America

Note: Market reaction is defined as movement in combined market capitalisation in the month following the merger announcement.
Source: Goldman Sachs estimates and company reports.

The sense of rapid and unexpected change in preferred models and success stories is painfully reflected in praise showered on First Union in an article in the July 1998 issue of *The Banker* by a banking consultant. Discussing the creation of value through mergers, he cites First Union as a success story:

> First Union, for example, is capable of digesting its prey within six months. No European bank can boast such an ability. How does First Union pull it off? The answer is that it has built an impressive capacity for assessing and integration acquisitions.[4]

As that article was written, First Union was comprehensively destroying value in its biggest acquisition to date.

So what conclusion can one draw on the likelihood of the bank merger 'bargain' remaining intact? Before answering this question, we should evaluate several other dimensions of the contract.

THE CHALLENGES OF CROSS-BORDER MERGERS

One such dimension is the trend in nature of merger transactions. As the mega-merger wave gains momentum, the transactions get bigger and, arguably, more complex and difficult to manage – as institutions like First Union have found to their sorrow. The really *new dimension at the outset of a new millennium, however, is that of cross-border mergers, which as we found in the previous chapter are now accepted as the logical next step in the European market.*

The evidence from experience to date in this new merger medium is limited but clear. Cross-border mergers add an extra dimension of complexity and execution risk. From the Chairman down the organisation chart, the message from our friends at MeritaNordbanken is that they require at a minimum a great deal of extra management time and effort to bridge national cultural boundaries. 'Europe' may be in the process of creation, and regions such as Iberia, Benelux and the Nordics may have much in common, but in the real world proximity breeds as much suspicion and antagonism as it does commonality. Whether it is Swedes against other Nordics, Portuguese against Spaniards, or Walloons against Flemings in Belgium, linguistic and cultural differences are a barrier to collaboration. As our friends at multinational banks like Fortis have said, in the fevered 'we and they' merger environment, it is only too easy to hide behind national culture to defend one's own interest. Emilio Ybarra, the Chairman of BBV, expresses the dilemma quite well in referring to his bank's 'preference zone' of southern Europe and the possibility of future mergers in those markets:

> There are technical difficulties. There are languages. There are supervisory bodies anxious not to lose their control.[5]

Equally important in the cross-border merger equation is the difficulty of generating cost savings to fit the stockholder value model. As we saw in Chapter 3, these are based on two pillars: closing down overlapping branches and the headquarters of one of the merging banks. In a cross-border merger, the first is physically impossible because of lack of overlap, while the second is usually out of the question for cultural reasons. One can only imagine the impact on MeritaNordbanken's morale if either the Stockholm or Helsinki headquarters were gutted or actually closed.

Over an extended time period, the strategic advantages of a cross-border fusion such as MeritaNordbanken may be overwhelming, but in raw stockholder value terms, as competitors like Lloyds TSB point out, the discounted present value of this future advantage does not add up. The model was built for the US, and the economics of US bank mergers generally remain attractive. But the model is only exportable to Europe and Japan with severe limitations.

For the European market, therefore, one can argue that the 'low-hanging fruit' of the merger process have largely been picked, and reaching into the higher branches of the tree for cross-border value is a risky business. There certainly remain attractive pickings in the rush to create national champions in Europe, but these will inevitably be limited by concerns over excess concentration and market power.

In Japan, the jury is out on the stockholder value to be created by bank mergers. The spate of merger announcements made in 1999 was driven by forces even more powerful than those impacting the US and European markets. Not only are Japanese banks facing the global issues of deregulation, overcapacity, heavy IT spending and low-cost competition, but they also must overcome a heritage of bad loans and, perhaps more important, modest earning power as measured against almost any other developed banking market.

Whether they will espouse the tenets of stockholder value as earnestly as they have other Western management doctrines is an open question. The potential for cost savings from integration is substantial, but so are the countervailing cultural forces against staff reduction. The most likely outcome is a version of the model used in European markets like Belgium and France where attrition and 'voluntary' early retirements are the principal vehicles for staff reduction. And a predilection for collective leadership could further undermine the potential merger gains.

HOW IMPORTANT IS SIZE?

Another key issue raised by the bank merger model is the relative importance of size or scale. Honest people can and do disagree honestly on this point, although most of them do so in defending their own strategic positioning. In our research one particular quotation rings a bell – that by David Daberko, CEO of the mid-sized and successful US regional bank National City Corporation in Cleveland:

> Bigger is better, all other things being equal. But all other things are rarely equal.[6]

Daberko, like other mid-sized US peers such as Fifth Third in Cincinnati, has prospered by acquiring relatively small, underperforming banks and bringing them up to National City's benchmarks.

In earlier chapters we have heard the praises of size sung by a variety of US and European bank executives. The counter-argument is well put by Tom Brown of Tiger Management:

> The diseconomies of management scale more than offset the economies of processing scale. As organisations expand their geographic range and product complexity, they inevitably become more difficult to manage. Their ability to adapt to market conditions also becomes impaired.[7]

On the other side of the Atlantic, Professor Herwig Langohr of INSEAD in Fontainebleau makes the same point:

> Complexity increases exponentially with product scope, customer base and geographic coverage. New co-ordination, monitoring and communication costs overlay rapidly the fixed costs associated with smaller size. In the end, average costs often increase.[8]

In our view, the primacy of size has been overblown by its advocates. As we discuss below in our vision of the future competitive battlefield, there is certainly a role for size as a critical success factor for banks like Bank of America expanding to create the first US bank with national retail coverage, or a global investment bank competing for global distribution. Yet for others such as Wells Fargo attempting to build a different bank, size can be a distinct negative. The final word on the issue of size comes from Ed Furash:

> Execution is far more important than size. Vision is not a matter of size, but of finding the right position for the strategy being persued. Entities of all sizes and specializations will thrive![9]

Will there be a role for the middle-sized bank, the segment which the barbell theory consigns to the dustbin? Most assuredly YES, as shown by the examples of Fifth Third and National City in the US and BCP and Bank of Scotland in Europe. For these banks, which distinguish themselves by superior client service, innovative distribution channels or judicious choice of business segments, size is only one of a number of variables.

WILL THE INTERNET TRANSFORM THE MERGER EQUATION?

One other ingredient should be injected into the stockholder value debate: the Internet and its transformation of bank distribution. As indicated in the previous chapter, many of our interviewees mentioned the Internet as a possible deterrent to paying full prices for what are essentially existing branch-based franchises. Yet none confirmed that his own bank's merger strategy would definitely be impacted by the threat of this franchise value disappearing.

Predictions of the death of the bank branch have been both frequent and premature over the past few decades. New technologies have repeatedly been discarded or absorbed into traditional structures. Yet none has had the potential power of the Internet to replace these distribution structures. While the pace of change is debatable, the direction is clear: bank profitability is heading south, and the value of existing consumer franchises is under threat, both from non-banks and those banks like Citigroup, MeritaNordbanken and Bank One who are pro-actively using the Internet to poach other bank's clients. Susan Sternglass Noble, a senior bank analyst for J. P. Morgan in London, sees the Internet transforming the merger equation:

> The issue is the value of an existing branch network. Do you need to merge? No one can answer that question yet, but the Internet in Europe will create a price war spreading from brokerage to mutual funds and eventually to credit cards. Traditional banks will have no choice but to transform their structure. Those ahead of the Internet curve can export their expertise but will need local partners. Can you be a partner without going through the hellish merger process?

The likely impact of the Internet on the bank merger model will be complex, and we find it difficult to draw any firm conclusions. In logic the Internet should reduce valuation parameters and possibly the attraction of buying an existing franchise. Arguably integration problems will be reduced by the diminished importance of the traditional distribution systems. Yet there is little sign to date that banks' appetite for expansion has been diminished by the prospect of value destruction of the target franchise.

THE TRADITIONAL MERGER VALUATION MODEL UNDER THREAT

As the new millennium opens, we suggest it is time to reassess the basis on which investors have appraised bank mergers.

In our analysis above we have seen how a variety of factors has chipped away at the model's edges. Our research has convinced us that investors and other constituencies seriously underestimate the true cost of mergers. Such hidden costs of mergers, the trend in Europe toward cross-border transactions, the possible impact of the Internet, the growing risk and cost of execution failure, and the period of time needed for organisational change to bear fruit – all argue for a move away from a valuation based on a simplistic estimate of cost saves in a period of perhaps two–four years.

There will continue to be cost-based transactions for which this formula is relevant. The combination of relatively high potential cost savings plus a skilled integration machine can certainly generate significant stockholder value.

But the perceptive investor would do well to construct his own model for the multitude of other deals. We would suggest that this alternative model be structured around the following issues:

- *Leadership*: is there a clear leader (or possibly leaders) with a track record of success in piloting similar mergers? If not, we suggest a significant discount be applied to projected merger gains.
- *Strategic positioning*: will the merger simply add together two (or more) organisations, or is there a likelihood that two and two will equal five – through cross-selling, achieving market dominance building the skills base, or improving competitive positioning? Such a question is particularly relevant for cross-border or so-called complementary mergers. As the consolidation wave continues, inevitably a significant number of deals will be those jammed together for defensive reasons or simply to create size.
- *Execution skills*: do the banks have a track record of successful merger execution, and is it likely they will execute efficiently? What is the likely cost and duration of integrating IT systems?
- *Financial synergies*: have the indicated synergies been appropriately discounted to take into consideration the downside risks of market share loss, an extended merger period, poor due diligence and loss of key staff?

So what conclusions can be drawn from this analysis of the bank merger model and the experience to date of our interview sample? How might this experience shape the future profile of the banking universe?

Our first conclusion is that the model as developed in the US with its focus on cost reduction in the near term has seen its best days – at least as applied in other markets like Japan and Europe.

Perhaps the greatest surprise from our interview series is the apparent inability of the due diligence process to provide a robust bulwark against inheriting 'nuclear waste' from one's merger partner. As long as the supply/demand imbalance in mergers continues, it is hard to see this situation changing. Thus any merger calculation under current circumstances should allow for nasty unexpected surprises.

The other hidden cost is the disruption inherent in the merger process. As this disruption is not as easily quantified as the apparent savings and revenue synergies, it will inevitably remain in the shadows. Yet investors must factor something into their stockholder value calculations. Finally, there is some evidence that many mergers ultimately fail to achieve the cost savings projected. Certainly outside the US and possibly inside as well, the cost-driven merger model has its limitations. Should the cross-border merger trend gather pace in Europe, a new valuation model will be essential. And a model for Japan should resemble that for a number of European countries where cost reduction is not an imperative.

WILL INVESTORS DRIVE A NEW BARGAIN?

How might the number and type of future deals evolve? Will the traditional merger model endure and the merger momentum of 1998–99 continue?

Any prediction in such a dynamic and complex environment is at best a hostage to fortune. Yet a few points can be made with some confidence. First, *if the merger bargain changes, it is likely to be investors who drive that change.* The bank merger boom of the late 1990s could not have taken place without enthusiastic support from the institutional investment community. Second, investors in US and European bank stocks have responded repeatedly to disappointing merger outcomes by savaging the unfortunate bank's stock. *Should they conclude that the old bargain is not realistic in a growing number of transactions for the reasons we have outlined, a new one might emerge.* Ed Furash describes a possible rationale:

Only a small handful of banks has learned how to handle large mergers successfully. Even those who apparently succeed have had some hidden problems. There's no perfect model, no precise way of doing it. You need strong leadership, the willingness of leader to pay attention to detail, and a strategy. Most merging banks don't have a strategy. They're opportunistic.

J.P. Morgan's Susan Sternglass Noble describes an investor universe marked by what she terms:

realistic cynicism. Banks must merge, but most investors believe they have mediocre management driven by egotism and political considerations. So realistically they don't expect perfect merger execution; you take the best you can get.

If investors buy the argument that a large and growing number of mergers are likely to fail to meet expectations because of a lack of leadership, poor execution, extended time period needed to show results, or any other factor we have discussed, the pace of consolidation and nature of transactions could also change. Transactions which promise to create a transformed institution led by a superlative CEO could be blessed despite the absence of significant short-term cost saves. Correspondingly, deals which simply slam together institutions without such leadership or realistic combined strategy might be met by an investor sell-off.

Whether or not a new model emerges, one can hope for a more sophisticated evaluation of merger announcements than in the past. One of our interviewees, a senior buy-side analyst for a major European bank, confirms that a typical response traditionally has been to 'buy on rumour and sell on the confirmation!' If our research has proven anything, it is that such knee-jerk reaction in bank mergers is naïve. A host of variables – leadership, structure, strategy, likely pace of execution, track record, cultural issues, IT problems – as well as the likely cost and revenue synergies must be factored into a intelligent investment decision.

A final word on the topic: Bob Yates and others have noted that today's market capitalisation game has given bank management currency which they have to spend to meet investor expectations. As Professor Haspeslagh of INSEAD points out, however:

The harsh truth is that merging by itself does not produce a world class company; it merely opens the door to opportunity.[10]

HOW MIGHT BANK MERGER STRATEGIES EVOLVE?

Despite the seemingly inexorable trend toward mega banking institutions, we believe strongly that banking in the future will be characterised by structural diversity. A variety of new merger models might gain prominence, while several existing formulae will survive.

As investor preferences evolve, some of today's champions of scale and scope might well reinvent themselves by spinning off lines of business – just as several North American and German banks have done with their e-commerce businesses. A broader de-consolidation or unbundling could well occur as investors demand a larger conglomerate discount in the face of superior performance by more focused institutions. One can easily envisage more universal banks spinning off their fund management, investment banking, private banking or other units to boost their aggregate market value.

Another model is the proposition put forward by the new Wells Fargo: a revenue-driven formula based on cross-selling retail products through a host of distribution channels to an existing customer base. Citigroup is another proponent of this solution, as are cross-selling veterans in Europe like BCP. The critical success factor for such Wal-Marts of the banking world will be carefully honed staff training, compensation and management information systems – which are not, sadly, strengths for most retail banking institutions.

Another will be the global product specialist. Banks across the world have witnessed the success of non-bank 'category killers' like Cetelem in consumer finance, Schwab in discount brokerage, GE Capital in equipment finance and credit cards, and Fidelity and Alliance Capital in fund management. In sectors like global custody and cash management, banks like Chase and Citibank have successfully won market share, and others should follow. The 'bulge group' of US investment banks has similarly achieved domination of the global securities and M & A businesses. Europe has seen relatively few of these focused success stories, but German Internet brokers like Con-Sors in the late 1990s show that there is room for change in markets hitherto dominated by massive universal banks.

As Pat Butler, Principal in McKinsey & Company's London financial institutions practice, sees the future:

The pressure will continue to build market capitalisation since in a rapidly globalising economy superior market cap is the ultimate offensive weapon. It gives you the strength to acquire the assets, to structure the alliances and to attract the talent needed to capture opportunities. But the particular route to superior market cap is important. The winners will be those who not only acquire but actively reshape their businesses. Essentially the successful banks will

Figure 13.4 Major disparities in European ROE by line of business might drive restructuring

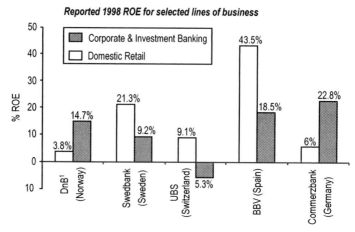

Reported 1998 ROE for selected lines of business

¹ RAROC *basis.*
Source: Company reports.

not only be big in a global sense but increasingly manage a portfolio of specialist businesses.

This business proposition closely resembles the formula recommended by interviewees such as Leonhardt Pihl of Den Danske Bank. It is enhanced in Europe by the sharp disparity in returns in European banks across national markets and client/product segments. Whereas in the US, ROEs by line of business generally fall into the 15–20 per cent range, in Europe they range from break-even to 40 per cent and more.

Figure 13.4 profiles these disparities in 1998 for five European banks who disclose returns by line of business – specifically domestic retail and corporate/investment banking.

Thus returns from domestic retail banking for the banks surveyed ranges from 4 per cent in Norway and 6 per cent in Germany to 44 per cent in a major Spanish bank, while corporate banking shows somewhat smaller variations. Such disparities could well justify consolidation on a line of business basis in European banking. A similar development has taken place in non-life insurance in Europe, where several Nordic competitors in this low-profit business have combined forces to reduce capacity and slash overheads.

Our universe includes several business models which should endure. One is that embodied by Lloyds TSB and Svenska Handelsbanken: the disciplined and focused acquirer which profits from opportunities to buy cheaply, sell off relatively unprofitable businesses, and execute transactions efficiently. Lloyds TSB's strategic focus reflects this discipline. While other banks talk about it, Lloyds TSB lives up to the statement in its 1998 annual report:

> Our strategy is to focus on selective market leadership and to avoid markets where, realistically, we cannot be among the best. We would rather be a leader in a few markets than a minor participant in many.

Another is the new bank – that rare animal where two plus two has indeed created five. Chase Manhattan and, hopefully, Wells Fargo fall in this category where strong leadership, an inclusive culture, and the ability to leverage professional skills and clients creates extra value. The revenue-driven profile described above is a variant of this model. Scepticism over the ability to create such a paragon is understandable, and many of the aspirants will fail in the attempt. Given sufficient time, a benign external environment and, above all, strong leadership, however, the goal is an achievable one.

A FINAL WORD

But none of these behavioural changes may occur. The consensus view, as well as today's bank merger model, may prevail. The dumbbell profile, dominated by a diminishing handful of mega-universal banks, may emerge, along with the oft-predicted demise of the mid-sized bank.

Yet even if this is the case, our findings from the interview series are still relevant. If we are indeed at the early stages of the bank merger endgame, investors and bank management would do well to apply more discipline and rigor to key decisions such as the selection of people and IT systems, to invest more in communicating the vision of the merger, and to select a CEO who can truly drive the difficult merger process. Due diligence might become a true safety net, and investors might be more rigorous in questioning the assumptions underpinning merger economies. At the same time, they may become supportive of mergers which will truly create a more competitive and better positioned 'new bank', albeit over a longer time frame than the merger period. As so many of our interviewees point out, agreeing a merger only creates the opportunity: successful execution achieves the actual value!

Appendix

The appendix which follows is designed to provide the background on the 33 banks interviewed. In addition to a brief profile on the bank itself, it analyses a specific major merger transaction which has taken place during the past decade, along with the strategic and financial targets established.

The sources for each of these profiles are the rating agency Fitch IBCA as well as company documents, in particular merger prospectuses.

ABN AMRO

Business Profile

> One of Europe's top 10 banks in asset terms, ABN Amro since its formation by merger in 1991 has expanded to become a truly global banking institution with operations in over 70 countries. Its home market of the Netherlands, where it has over 20% of bank loans and deposits, accounts for about 40% of total operating earnings, with the US, where it has strength in the Midwest, representing 34% of the total. The group is attempting to broaden its business base in Europe with a major commitment to Italy following unsuccessful acquisition attempts in France and Belgium. Its global investment banking business is anchored by a substantial market share in the Netherlands. ROE in recent years has approximated a satisfactory 12–14%

Major recent merger transactions

> The group was formed in 1991 by a merger of equals between Algemene Bank Nederland (ABN) and Amsterdam-Rotterdam Bank (AMRO). To ensure strong bonding between the two institutions, the initial management board was made up of all 14 members of the existing boards in equal numbers from both banks. In addition, at the outset equality was also maintained at the next management level with co-heads (one from each bank) responsible for each major unit. The initial chief executive was the former AMRO CEO, who was succeeded in 1992 by his counterpart at ABN. A total of four years was necessary to create a common retail banking platform.

(A) Strategic rationale

The merger was designed both to reduce costs in a classic in-market merger as well as create the basis for a much larger entity with the critical mass to compete in the new single market of Europe as well as abroad. ABN's international capabilities complemented AMRO's domestic strength.

(B) Financial targets

Cost savings were projected at 7% of the combined cost base by the end of the merger period to be derived in large part from a 9% staff reduction (15% of domestic staff). In addition, the group has set generic ROE (minimum 12%) and cost/income goals (62.5%). All targets have been met with the exception of the cost/income ratio which was impacted by reduced revenues from unexpectedly severe competition. The extended four-year merger period needed to develop a new retail banking system produced some market share losses.

ARGENTARIA

Business Profile

Spain's third largest banking group was formed in 1991 from the merger of five formerly government-owned banks, including the Caja Postal mass market retail bank, the Banco Hypotecario mortgage bank and the BEX wholesale/retail network. With a relatively limited retail branch network, the group has focused on innovative delivery systems and built market share in the asset management sector both in Spain and abroad in Latin America. Earnings performance has improved steadily as the cost base is reduced and the problem loans inherited from predecessor banks shrink. A new management team in 1996 has accelerated the integration process and merged the group's retail brands.

In October 1999, management announced an agreed merger with BBV.

Major recent merger transactions

The merger which formed the Argentaria group in 1991 brought together five banking institutions whose only common denominator was their government ownership. Management's immediate task was to deal with serious asset management problems during an economic downturn as well as take drastic steps to reduce the cost base and inject a profit-oriented culture. Argentaria decided to maintain the brands of its predecessor banks but not integrate IT systems and other central units.

A new management team in 1996 took steps to integrate systems and central functions and create a single Argentaria brand to reduce costs and minimise internal friction.

(A) Strategic rationale

The merger's rationale was to extract from the state-owned banking system those elements capable of functioning as profit-generating entities as well as create a larger competitor in anticipation of EC 92. Integrating and modernising these disparate units was a major management challenge both for the initial team and that taking over in 1996 – particularly during the economic downturn of the early 1990s. By maintaining its multiple brand strategy in the post-merger period, Argentaria avoided the market share loss suffered by some of its peers.

(B) Financial targets

No specific targets were set for the merger period. In any case, severe asset write-downs and other losses depressed earnings in 1995–97, and only in 1998 did ROE climb to an acceptable 12.8%, albeit still below the level of Argentaria's peers. An extended merger period of four years only ended in 1995, following which the new management team took a number of measures to integrate the group and reduce costs further.

Appendix

BANCO BILBAO VIZCAYA

Business Profile

> Banco Bilbao Vizcaya (BBV) is Spain's second largest bank, formed from a merger of equals in 1988. In recent years it has built a major presence by acquisition of controlling interests in eight Latin America countries, which account for roughly a quarter of total assets but a much smaller portion of earnings.
>
> It is Spain's second largest manager of mutual and pension funds with strength also in private banking, domestic investment banking and consumer credit.
>
> In October 1999, BBV announced a 'merger of equals' with the smaller number three Spanish bank, Argentaria; BBV's CEO will assume the same role in the merged entity. In recent years, BBV has initiated a regional expansion strategy focusing on Southern Europe, where it has taken a minority stake in Italy's Banca Nazionale del Lavoro.

Major recent merger transactions

> BBV was formed from the 1988 merger of equals of Banco de Vizcaya and Banco Bilbao to create at the time Spain's largest bank with about 20% of the retail market. Each of the predecessor banks had been highly regarded, and both of the former chief executives remained in place as co-heads with an agreement for the leadership to pass eventually to Vizcaya's Pedro Toledo. Even before M. Toledo's unexpected death, however, conflicts between executives from the two banks erupted with the result that the Bank of Spain was obliged to step in to name a single successor in the form of the number two from Bilbao, Emilio Ybarra, who currently remains in place.

(A) Strategic rationale

One of the earliest mergers made in anticipation of the Single European market in 1992, BBV's rationale was to create a major player on the European scene as well as achieve the significant cost economies which were seen as necessary for survival in the post-1992 environment. In fact, strategic priority was given first to expansion in Latin America and only recently to Italy.

(B) Financial targets

By reducing the number of branches by 10% in the first year (with smaller subsequent cuts) and reducing the number of staff by 1,000 (through attrition and negotiated retirements) annually for five years, BBV targeted a 15% overall staff reduction from the merger. These targets were achieved, but an extended and expensive investment in a new IT system helped to boost the cost/income ratio well above the pre-merger level, and only in 1995 did it fall to 56% against 60–70% during the merger period.

BANCO COMERCIAL PORTUGUES

Business Profile

Established *de novo* in the mid-1980s as a private sector bank competing with nationalised entities, Banco Comercial Portugues (BCP) has used a uniquely segmented distribution strategy to maximise revenue through strong cross-selling capabilities. With its 67%-controlled affiliate Banco Portugues do Atlantico, it is now the second largest bank in the country with market shares of 28% in fund management, 23% in life insurance and 17% in residential mortgages. Abroad, it has a well developed network of alliances with other European banks, and it has bid for control of the Mundial Confianza group which, if successful, would provide another 13% of banking market share.

Roughly 35% of group profits are derived from BPA, while the Nova Rede mid-market branch network contributes almost half of the parent bank's earnings.

Major recent merger transactions

The successful contested bid for BPA in 1996 has been the major corporate event for BCP since its formation. Rather than absorb the bank in an in-market merger, BCP retained the BPA brand and corporate structure and totally revamped its retail distribution network to create a separate distribution channel and thereby preserve BPA's client base. Common IT and other support services are provided by a central entity, ServiBanca. A minority stake in BPA was floated following the restructuring.

(A) Strategic rationale

While the BPA merger created a much larger bank with greater market shares in key business segments, another strategic objective was to maintain the group's combined market share by retaining each of its brands and identities. At the same time economies would be realised by the full merger of key product groups such as fund management and insurance and the development of a single banking platform. A key strategic objective has been to boost the cross-selling ratio in BPA to the level achieved by BCP.

(B) Financial targets

Only aggregate performance targets were set for the merger; a minimum return of 20% (calculated as BCP's cost of equity plus 50%) of the capital invested in BPA. In addition, we understand that 7–8% of the combined cost base was cut.

BANCO SANTANDER CENTRAL HISPANO

Business Profile

By far Spain's leading bank since its 1999 merger of equals, BSCH earns about 53% of its profit from domestic retail banking. It dominates the Spanish mutual fund market with a 24% share and has won a 20% commercial banking market share through pro-active and innovative marketing. Abroad, the group derives about 20% of its earnings from Latin America after the additional stakes acquired in certain subsidiaries, such as Banco Santiago in Chile. In addition, BSCH in Europe has adopted a strategy of strategic minority interests with banks in the UK (Royal Bank of Scotland), Italy (San Paolo IMI), Germany (Commerzbank) and France (Société Générale).

Major recent merger transactions

The merger of equals in April, 1999 of Banco Central Hispano and Banco Santander created Spain's leading bank. Learning from their earlier mergers in the decade, both banks agreed to move quickly to put in place a new strategy and structure and make key decisions such as the choice of IT platforms. To minimise market share loss at the expense of cost savings, all three retail brands (Banesto, Santander and BCH) will be retained. The CEO is the former Chief Executive of BCH.

(A) Strategic rationale

The managements of both predecessor banks are committed to increasing size and scale in a consolidating banking world. The merger will also generate significant in-market economies as well as boost market shares in key sectors such as mutual and pension funds. In addition, the merger reduces the relative importance of Santander's major investment in Latin America.

(B) Financial targets

The key financial target set for the merger is that of PTA 105 billion in cost savings, or 10% of combined costs (and 20% of Spanish costs) over the three-year merger period. Management at the time of the merger also committed itself to an ROE of 19–20% (vs. 16% in 1998), annual earnings growth of 25% per annum, and cost income ratio of 57% (vs. 62%).

BANK AUSTRIA

Business Profile

Bank Austria dominates the Austrian banking sector with a share of at least 20% in key products such as loans and deposits, corporate banking, fund management and investment banking. Given the low profitability of domestic banking and the development opportunities in neighbouring Central and Eastern European (CEE) markets, Bank Austria has expanded vigorously in the region and now is the second largest foreign bank in the CEE, where its ROE has approximated 25% against single digits in Austria.

Its overall strategy is to strengthen its domestic market share, reinforce the asset management business, expand in the CEE region and improve profitability by integration measures. The bank's strategy calls for increasing earnings from the CEE to 20% of the group total by 2001.

Major recent merger transactions

The take-over of Creditanstalt in 1997 by Bank Austria, who purchased the government's controlling stake, created Austria's dominant bank. As part of the deal, Bank Austria committed not to change the structure of Creditanstalt for five years. In practice, this has produced a complex corporate structure, which enables the two separate retail banking brands (Bank Austria and Creditanstalt) to function in the domestic market and Bank Austria Creditanstalt International to operate in the international and investment banking sectors. While a number of senior Creditanstalt executives left at the time of the merger, the current top 12 executives are roughly balanced between members of the two predecessor banks.

(A) Strategic rationale

The merger of Austria's first and second bank created a dominant player with leadership positions in corporate and retail banking and asset management as well as greater strength in CEE, which is viewed as the principal area for earnings growth.

(B) Financial targets

Merger goals are expressed in aggregate terms for the merger period ended in 2001: 12% ROE (against 11% in 1997), a cost income ratio of less than 60% (against 70%), earnings per share of Euro 5.81 (vs. 3.62) and an increase to 20% of the proportion of CEE earnings. Back office functions will be merged and a common IT platform installed by mid-2000. Cost savings are projected at 18% of the pre-merger total, including a substantial program initiated before the merger by CA and a reduction by attrition of 2,500 in staff.

BANK ONE CORPORATION

Business Profile

The fourth largest bank in the US with over $300 billion in assets at year-end 1998, Bank One was created in 1998 by the merger of Bank One in a merger of equals with First Chicago NBD Corporation, itself created by a similar merger in 1995. Its core geographic footprint is the Central and Southwest US with strength in retail as well as corporate banking. A major strategic thrust has been general purpose credit cards; by the 1997 purchase of the specialist First USA, Bank One has become the largest card issuer in the US with 27% of group earnings in 1998. Bank One distinguished itself in the early 1990s by an aggressive acquisition campaign which did not integrate the acquired entities but used best practice benchmarking in a program called 'the uncommon partnership' to maximise profitability. This programme, however, was reversed in the mid-1990s in favour of full integration.

Major recent merger transactions

In October, 1998, Bank One and First Chicago NBD consummated a merger of equals to create a super-regional bank with a broader geographic scope as well as a more diversified revenue base. John McCoy of Bank One was named Chief Executive Officer with Verne Istock of First Chicago NBD as Chairman.

In October 1999, following an earnings warning stemming from slower than anticipated growth in the group's core credit card business, Mr McCoy relinquished many of his day-to-day operating responsibilities to take direct oversight of the credit card business. In December 1999, he resigned from the bank.

(A) Strategic rationale

In addition to doubling the group's size and extending its branch network to a much larger portion (14 states) of Central and Southwest USA, the merger created a more balanced business profile. Commercial/corporate banking represents 25%, credit cards 27%, retail 18% and investment management 5% of total earnings.

(B) Financial targets

Over a two-year period, management estimates cost synergies of about 10% ($970 million) of the 1997 cost base with $275 million (2%) in revenue synergies. There was only a partial overlap in branch networks.

BANK OF TOKYO MITSUBISHI

Business Profile

One of Japan's leading banks and a key member of the prominent Mitsubishi Group, Bank of Tokyo Mitsubishi has the most diversified business profile of any of the major Japanese city banks. It has retained the leadership position in foreign exchange and international finance contributed by the former Bank of Tokyo with its operations in 43 overseas countries, while the former Mitsubishi Bank is one of the country's blue-chip domestic banks with over 300 branches. Its securities affiliate is one of the two leading bank-owned firms in the Japanese fixed income markets.

BTM's superior track record enabled it to remain the major Japanese bank not to request government financial assistance in 1999 to increase provisioning against problem loans. On the other hand, such provisions for BTM have more than offset operating income over the period 1996–99.

Major recent merger transactions

The merger of equals in 1996 between the international specialist BOT and domestically-oriented Mitsubishi Bank was the first such fusion since the 1971 formation of Dai Ichi Kangyo Bank. The top executives of each bank were largely retained in the new management team. While the overseas offices of the two banks in the same city were merged, there has been limited restructuring of the two entities to create a truly seamless organisation.

(A) Strategic rationale

Each of the two component banks felt the need to broaden its product and client base: BOT found itself facing strong competition in its niche of foreign exchange and trade finance, while Mitsubishi Bank needed a stronger international capability to meet its clients' needs. The broad Mitsubishi client base would be offered the international services of BOT, who could thus multiply its client reach.

(B) Financial targets

No financial targets were set specifically for the merger. Over the past few years, however, under the stimulus of greater competition, increased deregulation and, more recently, other major Japanese bank mergers, BTM has articulated more specific steps to increase stockholder value. Thus in September 1999, three years after the merger, a target ROE of 11% by 2002 was fixed. While not merger-specific, the bank's measures will focus on revenue generation and the reduction of central costs rather than staff reduction.

CHASE MANHATTAN CORPORATION

Business Profile

One of the largest US banking organisations, Chase has grown organically and by acquisition on a focused basis to achieve leadership in a number of targeted businesses. It derives about 70% of earnings from its global banking unit, which includes leading franchises in foreign exchange and derivatives trading as well as syndicated lending and corporate banking activities in the US. The balance comes from Chase's leading 23 per cent stake in retail banking in the NY Tri-state area, its national credit card and mortgage franchises and major positions in global custody and cash management. The product of 1991 and 1996 mergers within the NY money centre banking community, Chase has achieved enviable results from these mergers in terms of cost saves, revenue generation, and resource allocation. The major remaining strategic challenge is to build a balanced investment banking capability, and the 1999 acquisition of the Hambrecht & Quist equity specialist is a major step in that direction.

Major recent merger transactions

The 1996 merger of equals between the old Chase and Chemical Bank built on the successful model of Chemical's 1991 merger with Manufacturer's Hanover. Led by the former Chemical's CEO who had also directed the ManHan merger, the new bank aggressively employed profit measurement techniques such as stockholder value added (SVA), perfected risk management strategies based on VaR and stress testing to improve the risk reward ratio, and divested low-profit businesses. Its success in improving stockholder value while at the same time retaining key staff from the merged banks has made Chase a role model in successful US merger execution.

(A) Strategic rationale

The Chase/Chemical merger aimed at achieving economies of investment in IT as well as significant operating economies from overlap in retail banking in the NY area and businesses such as global cash management and custody and credit cards where both banks were active.

(B) Financial targets

Cost savings from the merger were estimated at 18% of the combined banks' expense base and 38% of the smaller bank (Chase), primarily from central corporate and IT functions. Total cost saves were estimated at $1.5 billion, including the closure of 200 branches and a 12,000 reduction in employee base. In addition, an aggregate ROE target for the merged group was set at 18% (against an actual 13% in 1996).

Chase has achieved the indicated savings and reported an 18% ROE for 1998.

CITIGROUP

Business Profile

Citigroup is the product of a merger of equals in 1998 between Citicorp and the Travelers Group to create the largest financial company in the US with over $650 billion in assets. The former Citigroup boasted the largest overseas network of any bank, with particular strength in Asia and Latin America, strength in global corporate banking (including leadership positions in foreign exchange and global custody) and a major global retail bank. The Travelers group contributed a broad range of domestic US retail financial services, including life and non-life insurance and consumer finance, and the Salomon Smith Barney investment bank. The combined entity derives 48% of its earnings from its global consumer business and 36% from global investment banking. As a result of the merger, the level of US earnings has risen from 45 to roughly 70% of the total.

Major recent merger transactions

In October 1998 the merger of equals of Travelers Group and Citigroup was consummated. It is unique in such transactions in its corporate governance: the chief executives of the merging institutions remain co-chief executives of the merged entity, while other key positions in the management group were also given to co-heads. Only in July 1999 was a delineation of some responsibilities between the co-chief executives announced. Subsequent to the merger there have been a number of changes in the senior executive team, including the departure of the individual widely viewed as the successor to the two co-chief executives.

(A) Strategic rationale

The merger's rationale centres on cross-selling of both retail and corporate financial services. In the retail sector, the Travelers' successful dynamic marketing strategy for financial services will be applied to the retail client base of Citigroup, which had not been known for its cross-selling capabilities, while in the investment banking realm the Salomon Smith Barney investment bankers are expected to cross-sell with Citibank corporate bankers. Close integration of the operating units themselves is not regarded as essential to the merger's success.

(B) Financial targets

No specific financial targets have been established as incremental gains from the merger. On the other hand, overall ROE and revenue targets for the merged group have been set, and, to date, met, while the group is proceeding with plans to reduce its expense base.

CREDIT AGRICOLE

Business Profile

The largest banking group in France as well as Europe in asset terms, Credit Agricole is a mutual co-operative owned by its members grouped within regional *caisses regionales*. It dominates the French retail market with 16 million retail clients, about 8,000 branches of the regional *caisses*, and roughly 20–25% of key segments such as domestic deposits and loans as well as consumer finance. Its life insurance and fund management arms have a smaller share (roughly 10%) of the French market.

Through its acquisition of Indosuez, the group now has a wide international network with strength in Asia as well as a significant corporate banking and investment banking activity. Its retail placing power gives the group a major support for its French capital market operations.

Major recent merger transactions

In July 1996 Credit Agricole acquired from the Compagnie de Suez group Banque Indosuez, a wholesale and international bank active in over 60 countries with particular strength in corporate banking in the Middle East and Asia, project finance, capital markets and stockbrokerage. From the outset, Indosuez and Credit Agricole's corresponding units were merged on a line of business basis and renamed Credit Agricole Indosuez (CAI). Subsequent to the merger, significant losses were suffered by CAI in 1997 and 1998 in Asia and Russia.

(A) Strategic rationale

The Indosuez merger fulfilled a long-standing desire on the part of Credit Agricole management to extend its business model to the domestic and international corporate banking and capital markets segments following unsuccessful efforts to reach the critical size organically. Indosuez offered a unique opportunity to acquire this market position at a reasonable price from Suez.

(B) Financial targets

No specific financial targets were set for incremental gains from the merger, but a goal of 12% ROE was established for the combined CAI. Due to credit and market losses since then, the goal has not yet been achieved.

CREDIT SUISSE GROUP

Business Profile

One of the two dominant Swiss-based universal banking groups with 1998 assets of over $ 100 billion, Credit Suisse Group (CSG) is made up of its CSPBBU private banking unit (which accounts for over 50% of earnings and is one of the world's largest); the CSFB global investment bank and the Credit Suisse domestic banking arm. Having in recent years suffered from global market volatility in the investment banking business as well as the marginally profitable domestic Swiss banking business, CSG has recently returned to levels of significant profitability. Following a 1997 restructuring, CSFB has confirmed its role as a major global investment banking competitor, while private bank CSPBBU with around 300,000 clients and over SF 400 billion under management is also a global player. In 1997, the group acquired Winterthur, a leading international insurer based in Switzerland, which had been the object of an unfriendly take-over bid.

Major recent merger transactions

The merger of Credit Suisse and Winterthur in 1997 created the first Swiss *bancassurance* group. Winterthur, which was roughly one-third the size of CS, has retained its own corporate structure and independent Board of Directors, with its CEO joining the CSG board. At the retail level, in 80 domestic regions, bank and insurance branches collaborate to cross-sell each other's products, while CSG's life subsidiary has been sold to Winterthur. We believe, however, that actual collaboration has been limited, in part at least because of the merger commitment to separate structures.

(A) Strategic rationale

The merger was triggered by an apparent unfriendly take-over bid for Winterthur, which had been CS's strategic insurance partner in Swiss and other markets. While CS management had earlier indicated that it was not necessary to own its insurance provider, a defensive merger was agreed. In addition, efforts would be made to cross-sell their respective products in the Swiss market.

(B) Financial targets

Relatively modest synergies were projected for the domestic linkage between the two groups. Cost synergies of less than 1% of the total were estimated from sharing IT and premises expense, while comparable revenue synergies were projected from cross-selling insurance products in the bank network.

DEN NORSKE BANK

Business Profile

> Norway's largest financial institution, Den norske Bank has a leadership
> position in the Norwegian capital and foreign exchange markets, a 25% share
> of Norway's corporate banking business and roughly a 15% retail market
> share. It was one of the first European banks to acquire control of a life
> insurance company, Vital, in 1996, and has recently acquired Postbanken, a
> retail bank selling through post-office branches.
>
> Formed in 1990 by the merger of equals between Den norske Creditbank
> and Bergen Bank, DnB emerged from the banking crisis with a significant
> holding by the Norwegian government, which has indicated its intent to
> continue to hold at least a one-third minority interest.

Major recent merger transactions

> DnB's formation in 1990 from the merger of two of Norway's leading banks was
> based on swift execution, significant staff cuts, and a selective approach to the
> formation of the new top management team (as opposed to the frequently
> employed formula of simply bringing together the existing top teams). The
> former CEO of Bergen Bank became the new bank's chief executive, and the
> systems merger took only six months because of the common use of IBM
> systems among the Norwegian banks.

(A) Strategic rationale

This classic in-market merger
generated both significant
economies as well as by far the
country's largest bank in
anticipation of EU 92. While the
bank was overtaken by the
Norwegian banking crisis in 1992
which placed DnB under
government ownership, it has
retained the role of the country's
dominant financial institution. The
banking crisis derailed tentative
plans to merge with other leading
Nordic banks in the Scandinavian
Banking Partners Group.

(B) Financial targets

Like other Scandinavian banks at
the time, financial goals for the
merger were expressed in terms of
cost savings. Within two years,
staff numbers would be cut by
13–14%, total operating expenses
over the same period would be
reduced by 9–13%, and the number
of domestic branches would be cut
by 17% during the first year. The
banking crisis intervened during
this period and accelerated the cost
reduction process.

DEUTSCHE BANK

Business Profile

Following the 1999 acquisition of Bankers Trust, Deutsche Bank has become the world's largest bank with over $700 billion in assets. Although it only commands 5–6% of its home banking market, it also has extensive branch networks in Italy and Spain and is actively acquiring a retail presence in other European markets.

Given the constraints on profitable growth in Germany and its traditional role as a major corporate bank, Deutsche has determined that its strategic development will largely take the form of expansion in global investment banking as well as fund management and corporate services such as global custody, each of which was reinforced by the Bankers Trust transaction. Its double strategic challenge is to win market share in this highly competitive business as well as boost group profitability to competitive levels.

Major recent merger transactions

By paying $9 billion (roughly one-third of its own market cap) for Bankers Trust in 1999, Deutsche Bank has made a major strategic investment both in the global investment banking business as well as the US market, global fund management and corporate services such as global cash management and custody. It has been made clear that BT is being acquired and is being integrated into the existing DB line-of-business structure. A speedy merger process is one of the strategies designed to dispel the widespread scepticism over cross-cultural mergers in the investment banking sector and the obvious strains this has created within Deutsche Bank.

(A) Strategic rationale

The strategic rationale is to combine DB's existing investment banking strengths in areas like fixed income with BT's equity, high yield and other skills. At the same time DB will gain entry to the US corporate banking on a major scale. Substantial synergies are expected from removing investment banking overlap as well as winning market share in strategic businesses such as global custody and cash management and fund management.

(B) Financial targets

Key merger targets include gross cost savings of roughly DM 2 billion, or 10% per annum, mainly through a reduction in staff of 5,000 outside Germany. In addition, on a group basis DB's ROE target is 25% pre-tax (against 6% on an adjusted basis in 1998). A major challenge in achieving this goal will be to reduce the cost/income ratio (78% in 1998) while at the same time investing to compete successfully with the US bulge group investment banks.

DEXIA

Business Profile

> The largest provider of finance to public sector entities in Europe, Dexia was created in 1996 by the merger of the dominant French and Belgian specialists in this sector. Largely through the acquisition route, Dexia now also has operations in Spain, Austria, Italy and Germany – often through joint ventures with local partners. The group currently has a market share in Europe of 10% of public sector finance. In addition, the group aims to build a major capability in fund management and private banking, while in Belgium it also has 15% of retail banking deposits. The group is also active in project finance.
>
> In late 1999, Dexia simplified its corporate structure (which had involved two national holding companies each owning 50% of the operating companies) by the creation of a single quoted holding company to enable the group, among other things, to make larger acquisitions.

Major recent merger transactions

> The formation of Dexia in 1996 was a merger of equals between two formerly public sector entities – Credit Local in France and Credit Communal Belgique in Belgium – to create a dominant entity in European public sector finance. The group is still managed by a quadrumvirate (*comité consortial*) composed of two executives from each of the two original partners, who have a central staff but permit the operating units to function with a minimum of integration. The recent corporate restructuring will simplify the group's corporate governance.

(A) Strategic rationale

> Dexia's strategy is to use its capital base to grow revenues as well as expand geographically (across Europe) and functionally (into fund management and private banking). It acknowledges that significant cost reduction is unrealistic in the environment of its two home countries. Among other purchases, acquisitions of major stakes in banking institutions in Spain (Banco de Credito Local) and Italy (Crediop) have taken place.

(B) Financial targets

> No specific financial targets were set at the outset in 1996, although management points out that subsequently ROE has been sustained (at 12% in 1998 against 11% in 1996) and that no dilution per share has taken place.

DEN DANSKE BANK

Business Profile

Denmark's largest bank with over 30% of total banking assets and particular strength in corporate banking, Den Danske Bank (DDB) has also committed itself to a regional role in the Nordic market. In recent years it has acquired regional banks in Sweden (Ostgota Enskilda Bank) and Norway (Fokus Bank) as well as stockbrokers in Norway, Finland and Sweden.

In its home market it is a major player in the life insurance sector with an 18% market share, in large part from the absorption of what is now the Danica life insurer as a result of the collapse of one of the bank's borrowers.

Major recent merger transactions

DDB was formed in 1990 from a three-way merger of Den Danske Bank of 1871, Copenhagen Handelsbank and the regional bank Provinsbanken. With the former Den Danske clearly the dominant entity as well as providing the chief executive, the merger was completed in the relatively short time frame of two years, which was particularly important given the current banking crisis. The presence of three merger partners actually facilitated the merger process by providing a decisive vote on key issues. Every effort was made to select the top management on a meritocratic basis, with most of the top executives of the three banks remaining for the merger period.

(A) Strategic rationale

The merger was designed both to build scale in anticipation of EU 92 and the Single Market as well as reduce costs significantly.

(B) Financial targets

The principal financial targets were cost-related. The number of branches would be cut by 20%, head count would be reduced by 10% over the merger period by normal attrition and economies without forced layoffs, and overall costs would be kept flat over the 1990–91 merger period. These targets were all met, and an additional 20% staff reduction was announced after the merger period ended.

ERSTE BANK der oesterreichischen Sparkassen AG (Erste Bank)

Business Profile

Austria's second largest bank in asset terms, Erste Bank was formed in 1997 by the merger of Die Erste, major savings bank, with GiroCredit Bank, a wholesale institution providing central services to the country's savings banks. Its strategic focus is to maximise the profitability of its own retail network, provider value-added services to about 70 independent Austrian savings banks and extend its core business into neighbouring countries in Central and Eastern Europe. Its ROE of 11% in 1998 reflects the relatively low profitability of Austrian banking. The bank has a roughly 10% share of customer deposits and 27% of retail fund management in Austria. It is a quoted company whose largest single stockholder with 43% of the capital is the foundation AVS.

Major recent merger transactions

In October 1997, following the merger which created the larger Bank Austria group, control of GiroCredit, which had been in the hands of Bank Austria, was sold to Die Erste, which then merged the two organisations on a line of business basis. The merger thus brought together a wholesale institution active in the domestic and international capital and wholesale lending markets as well as fund management, and a major retail bank with a nation-wide network.

(A) Strategic rationale

The merger created a more powerful rival to Bank Austria as well as one with a better balance between retail and wholesale banking businesses. The group at end-1998 had a leading share of 27% of Austrian retail mutual funds.

(B) Financial targets

No targets were set for specific synergies from the merger. An overall ROE goal of 12% for the year 2000 (against 11% for 1998) with a lower cost income ratio (65–67%) and combined operating savings of ATS 1 billion were also established for the combined organisation.

FIRST UNION CORPORATION

Business Profile

The sixth largest US bank in asset terms at year-end 1998, First Union has grown aggressively, largely by acquisition, both in geographic 'footprint' as well as product range. Over 70 bank acquisitions in the Eastern US have created the largest consumer bank in this region, with particular strength in Florida, North Carolina, Pennsylvania and New Jersey, which contributes about 34% of net income. Capital markets, which constitute another 32% of earnings, stem from the acquisition of regional brokerage firms such as Wheat First and Everen as well as a number of fund managers. First Union is thus a leader in middle market M & A as well as fund management, where its $160 billion of assets, including $75 billion in mutual funds, ranks it among the leaders among commercial banks. In its efforts to build a broadly based national franchise, management has invested heavily in a retail banking platform to accommodate future acquisitions.

Major recent merger transactions

The April 1998 acquisition of the $48 billion Core States franchise in Philadelphia constitutes by far the largest and, in retrospect, most difficult expansion move made by First Union. Having paid five times book value for Core States, management decided upon an aggressive time frame and cost reduction programme to achieve the value promised stockholders. Customer losses well in excess of the norm substantially reduced anticipated revenues and, along with disappointing results from another recent acquisition, The Money Store, produced several earnings warnings in 1999 and the departure of the COO of First Union Corporation.

(A) Strategic rationale

Paying a premium price for the Core States business, the dominant bank in Eastern Pennsylvania, was deemed necessary to expand significantly First Union's geographic coverage in the mid-Atlantic area, where the bank was already present. Thus significant branch overlap existed to justify an aggressive cost reduction programme.

(B) Financial targets

The key financial target was an estimated 40% reduction of Core States' cost base to be achieved by a 12 month integration programme, 7,000 job cuts and 150 branch closings.

In practice, it was clear by the end of 1998 that a combination of departures of key Core States client-facing staff, unhappy customers and the need to devote scarce resources to a concurrent total revamp of First Union systems had produced revenue losses estimated at above the 5–10% normal in an in-market merger.

Several earnings warnings were given during the year 1999, and the bank's stock price fell about one-third from its historical high.

FLEET BOSTON CORPORATION

Business Profile

The eighth largest US bank in asset terms following its merger with Bank Boston Corp. in late 1999, Fleet is the dominant bank in the north-eastern US with national distribution in mortgage banking, student loan processing, investment services, commercial finance and commercial banking. It has grown largely by acquisition from modest origins in Providence, Rhode Island and by diversification, also by acquisition, into non-bank financial services. Through the merger with Bank Boston, Fleet has inherited a highly profitable Latin American banking franchise in Argentina and Brazil which accounts for 9% of pro-forma net income. Its Quick & Reilly discount brokerage firm is the third largest in the country, while its asset management arm manages over $120 billion in assets.

Major recent merger transactions

The merger with Bank Boston in the fourth quarter of 1999 ended a long series of negotiations over the future of the leading bank in Massachusetts. The combined market share in this state was so high that the Justice Department required Fleet to sell off 270 branches. The merged group's chief executive officer will be Fleet's Terry Murray until year-end 2001 when Bank Boston's CEO, Chad Gifford, will assume that role. The group's headquarters will be in Boston, and six of the top eight management jobs will be held by executives of the former Fleet. A 13% premium over Bank Boston's recent price was paid.

(A) Strategic rationale

The merger of the two largest banks in New England creates a position of true market power in this attractive region.
Diversification is also achieved by reducing Bank Boston's exposure to Latin America and giving its stockholders exposure to Fleet's national businesses.

(B) Financial targets

A total of 5,000, or 8% of the pro-forma total staff will be cut to achieve a roughly similar percentage reduction in operating expenses. Presumably a much higher reduction will take place in the overlapping market area.

FORENINGSSPARBANKEN (SWEDBANK)

Business Profile

Sweden's largest retail bank (and third largest overall) with a dominant share of at least 30% in core products such as deposits, loans and fund management, Swedbank has expanded also outside Sweden to build a presence – generally through minority interests – in what it terms the 'Balticum' – Northern Europe including the rest of the Nordic countries as well as the Baltic nations and Poland. Formed originally from the merger in the early 1990s of the country's major regional savings banks, Swedbank in 1997 merged with the smaller Foreningsbanken, which had itself been formed by the country's regional co-operative banks. Roughly 31% of group profits are accounted for by its mortgage subsidiary Spintab, with another 15% from fund management and insurance combined.

In late 1999, the bank's chief executive resigned due to apparent disagreement over strategy.

Major recent merger transactions

The merger in November 1997 of the old Swedbank with Foreningsbanken served not only to win market share and achieve synergies but also as a vehicle to transform the new group's culture, efficiency and technology. All employees over the age of 57 were offered a pre-retirement package, although many had to be rehired to fill necessary posts. In addition, all other employees who felt they could not subscribe to the new vision were offered training and the opportunity to leave by the end of 1999. The bank's stock fell sharply when investors became aware of the heavy net investment costs which accompanied the merger.

(A) Strategic rationale

The addition of the Foreningsbanken network increased Swedbank's retail market share to over 30%, although 144 branches were sold to independent savings banks and another 240 closed. As indicated above, to upgrade the merged bank's efficiency and customer service capability, almost 30% of the pre-merger staff were offered training and redundancy or pre-retirement packages and left the bank. In addition, a multiple of the annual merger savings was invested in technology, market development, training and overseas alliances.

(B) Financial targets

Cost economies of SKR 1.5 billion per annum, or 13.6% of the 1996 cost base, were indicated. Investors were not aware, however, of the extended time period needed to realise these savings or the other costs, indicated above, made to transform the bank. Some market share has also been lost as a result of the magnitude of the personnel and structural change in the retail system, while the bank's reported cost/income ratio actually increased to 69% in 1998 from 54% in 1996.

Appendix

FORTIS GROUP

Business Profile

Formed in 1990 by the merger of the Dutch insurer AMEV with the Dutch savings bank VSB and the Belgian insurer AG, Fortis has grown organically and by acquisition to become the major *bancassurance* group (selling insurance through bank branches) in the Benelux region and one of the top 15 European financial institutions by market capitalisation. Following the 1998 acquisition of Générale Bank in Belgium which gave the group a dominant 30% share of that banking market, a total of 60% of 1998 pre-tax earnings are derived from banking with 40% from insurance. In addition, Fortis commands a 21% share of the fund management market in the Benelux region. A recent reorganisation along functional lines has replaced the old geographic structure. Ownership in the group is held through two quoted holding companies in Belgium and the Netherlands.

Major recent merger transactions

The acquisition of Générale Bank in 1998 was a major step in the group's structure as well as building its total asset size. The purchase was negotiated with the seller of a major block of stock, although an unsuccessful counter bid by ABN Amro was supported by a number of the members of senior management. The old Générale Bank, which was the leading corporate bank in Belgium, has been merged with the group's existing Belgian and Dutch banks to form Fortis Bank, one of the two functional pillars of the group along with Fortis Insurance.

(A) Strategic rationale

Having already acquired a major savings bank, ASLK/CGER, in Belgium, the purchase of Générale Bank offered Fortis the opportunity to become by far the largest bank in the country with a 30% market share as well as bulk up the banking portion of the group and expand considerably its market capitalisation. Significant revenue gains are anticipated by applying the successful cross-selling techniques employed by ASLK/CGER.

(B) Financial targets

In addition to estimated revenue synergies of Euro 250 million, after the integration period of four years Fortis expects to cut staff by roughly 5,000 and Générale's costs by Euro 350 million – in effect reducing Générale's cost base by 10–12%.

HYPOVEREINSBANK

Business Profile

HypoVereinsbank (HVB) is Germany's second largest bank as well as Europe's leading mortgage lender. While it has only a 4% overall commercial banking market share in Germany, it boasts an 11% share of the German residential mortgage market. Internationally, the bank's strategy is become the first 'European bank of the regions' by replicating its success in the Bavarian market in Germany. In 1998, it made its first acquisition – FGH Bank, a Dutch commercial mortgage lender – and acquired control of the Polish bank BPH.

In addition to the home and commercial mortgage business which accounts for 75% of profits, HVB has targeted the fund management sector, where it is a major player with roughly DM 200 billion of assets under management including those of its UK-based affiliate, Foreign & Colonial.

Major recent merger transactions

The merger of equals which brought together the two Munich-based regional banks Bayerische Vereinsbank and Bayerische Hypotheken Bank was the first major bank merger in Germany in decades. The commitment was made to run the group on a line-of-business basis under the leadership of the former CEO of Vereinsbank. Shortly after the merger was completed in October 1998, management revealed the provision of DM 3.5 billion to cover anticipated losses from Hypo's real estate lending in the former East Germany. Subsequent to an independent audit, in October 1999 all of the former Hypo executives resigned from the HVB management board.

(A) Strategic rationale

The merger's strategic objectives were to achieve substantial economies from the merger of two overlapping networks as well as position the bank with sufficient market capitalisation to play a role in the consolidation of European banking. In addition, the larger bank could win market share in attractive growth areas like fund management and mortgage banking.

(B) Financial targets

The merger goals were well defined: a 15% after tax ROE (against 9% in 1997), a cost/income ratio of 50% against 60% (in 1996) and DM 1 billion in estimated savings (14% of the combined 1996 cost base) largely by reducing the number of branches by 20%.

While the planned synergies are being achieved, earnings have fallen well below target because of continued high loan loss provisions.

Appendix

ING GROUP

Business Profile

One of the original European *bancassurance* mergers, ING Group has grown organically and by acquisition since its formation in 1991 to become one of the largest European financial institutions measured by market capitalisation. Pre-tax earnings in recent months have been roughly balanced between banking and insurance, while about two-thirds of earnings stem from the Netherlands. In the banking sector, in recent years ING has acquired Banque Bruxelles Lambert in Belgium and BHF Bank in Germany. The third functional leg of the group, asset management, was responsible for €253 billion at the end of 1998. The group's investment banking business has been built around the acquisition of Barings, acquired following its failure in 1995. Since its origins ING has managed its units on a federal basis with limited operational integration and the preservation of most of the original brands.

Major recent merger transactions

The most significant merger transaction of the group was its formation as a merger of equals in 1991 from the fusion of the largest Dutch insurance group, Nationale Nederlanden, and the country's third largest bank, NMB Postbank. While organised under functional units which bring together banking, insurance and fund management entities, these entities have continued to function operationally much as they did before becoming part of ING. The group's chief executive has traditionally alternated between a banking and insurance executive, and efforts are made to keep the balance between these elements roughly equal.

(A) Strategic rationale

The merger was designed to create a much larger entity able to use its capital to acquire other financial institutions as well as benefit from the synergies between banking and insurance. ING Bank in the Netherlands now represents the largest single distribution channel for NatNed life products, and extensive collaboration takes place between bank and insurance entities in markets such as Central and Eastern Europe.

(B) Financial targets

The merger was not designed to reduce costs. Since its origins, the group has set aggregate targets such as ROE (a premium above the cost of funds), annual earnings growth and cost/income ratios.

KAPITAL HOLDING

Business Profile

Kapital Holding groups the Realkredit Danmark mortgage specialist with BG Bank, which itself is composed of the former Bikuben savings bank and the GiroBank giro payment institution. Unlike its larger peers, BG moved relatively late into the now deregulated mortgage sector, whereas the two larger banks have won significant market share with their own offerings. Bikuben was the country's largest savings bank with a 10% market share while GiroBank provided payment services through the Danish postal system. The merger with Realkredit replaces a strategic alliance with another mortgage provider, Nykredit, who had been BG's largest single stockholder.

In late 1999, Kapital bid unsuccessfully for FIH, a Danish industrial lender. Subsequently the group's chief executive resigned after a disagreement with the Board of Directors over the merger bid.

Major recent merger transactions

The 1998 merger of Realkredit Danmark with BG Bank was, like that of BG Bank itself, a complementary merger designed to build a larger institution without extensive operational integration. Realkredit continues to sell most of its mortgage products through other channels, including those of BG's banking competitors, thus creating internal competition within the group. Each of the three operating units continues to use its own operating systems, although there is some co-ordination at the holding company level.

(A) Strategic rationale

Having decided not to merge with its stockholder Nykredit to build market share in the key mortgage product, BG Bank merged with Realkredit to achieve that objective as well as build critical mass to compete with the two larger Danish banks. As former Realkredit stockholders own a major share of the merged group and Realkredit sells most of its product outside the BG Bank, assimilation measures are not a high priority.

(B) Financial targets

For a variety of legal and other reasons, effective integration of the mortgage bank and commercial bank is quite limited. Targeted savings amount to only DKR 200 million, or 3.5% of the combined cost base, and are limited to headquarters costs. Realkredit will retain its own corporate structure and operating systems as well as brand.

KBC BANKING AND INSURANCE (KBC)

Business Profile

KBC is the second largest Belgian financial group, with particular strength in the Flanders region, following its three-way merger in 1998. Through its multiple distribution channels involving both bank branches, independent insurance agents and brokers, the group controls 20–25% of the country's loan and deposit markets as well as 10% of the insurance sector. Insurance accounted for 23% of consolidated profits in 1998 with commercial banking for 35% and fund management for 21%. In addition, the group dominates the Belgian securities sector with a 21% market share.

Abroad, KBC has moved aggressively through strategic alliances and acquisitions to establish operating units in China, the Czech Republic, Hungary and Poland. International lending accounted for 44% of the loan book in 1998.

Major recent merger transactions

KBC was formed by the effective merger in 1998 of three entities effectively controlled by Flemish interests grouped around the Almanij holding company: Kredietbank (a major commercial bank), ABB (a mutual insurer) and Cera Bank, an agricultural co-operative. The dominant merger partner is the former Kredietbank, whose CEO became that of the new group, although the top 18 management jobs have been shared equally among the three partners. An extended four-year merger period is needed to build a new retail system on the back of the Cera system.

(A) Strategic rationale

The ultimate strategic rationale of the complex merger was to grow and retain the independence, in a rapidly consolidating market, of a champion for the Flemish financial interests. Ultimate control of KBC remains in the hands of these interests. In addition, the group increased its market shares in key domestic segments and created a vehicle for expansion in other markets.

(B) Financial targets

The only financial target set in relation to the merger itself has been an initial estimate of BF 50 billion in net present value from the merger (net of estimated revenue losses). This is equivalent to about 8% of the 1997 pro forma expense base. A total of 600 of the group's 1,500 branch units will be merged, while cross-selling will be encouraged by physically linking banking to insurance offices. There will be no forced layoffs but staff have been required to be flexible in terms of job location and function.

LANDESBANK BADEN-WUERTTEMBERG (LBBW)

Business Profile

Formed at the beginning of 1999 by the merger of three public sector banks in the prosperous German state of Baden- Wuerttemberg, LBBW is the dominant bank in the region and one of the top ten in Germany. It is unique in bringing together a retail bank (the former Landesgirokasse) as well as wholesale entities while still retaining the support guarantees offered by its public sector owners.

At least in part because of its profitable 231-unit retail branch network, LBBW's ROE at 10% in 1998 is much higher than its public sector peers. In addition to its retail business, LBBW has a significant capital markets activity and acts as the house bank for the governments of BW and Stuttgart as well as the central institution for the region's savings banks.

Major recent merger transactions

The three-way merger in 1999 between Landesgirokasse, Sudwestdeutsche Landesbank (the central institution of the regional savings banks) and the commercial business of L-Bank was the culmination of extensive negotiations which have taken place over many years among the political authorities in the state of BW as well as its publicly-owned savings banks. The strong influence of these authorities is reflected in the decision to rotate the Chairmanship of the bank every two years among executives of the three predecessor banks. A strategy is being developed with the assistance of outside consultants.

(A) Strategic rationale

The merger creates a major entity in the state of BW uniting its public sector banks and based in its capital Stuttgart. In the context of the on-going consolidation of the landesbank sector, it is envisaged that LBBW can play a more significant role in this consolidation as well as eventually achieve consolidation economies.

(B) Financial targets

No specific financial targets have been set for the merged group, although it would appear that few can be anticipated in the next few years because of the decision to continue to run three separate IT platforms for the foreseeable future.

LLOYDS TSB GROUP PLC

Business Profile

Only fifth in asset terms, Lloyds TSB leads its UK banking peers in most performance indicators and has earned a global reputation for the disciplined exercise of the stockholder value principle. Lloyds has focused on the retail financial services sector with a particular emphasis on mortgage lending, where it ranks third in the UK with roughly 10% of the market, and the sale of life and non-life products to bank customers, which accounts for 22% of earnings. The retail sector accounts for over 70% of earnings, with the balance derived from domestic wholesale banking (18%) and limited overseas operations in New Zealand and South America. Lloyds TSB has earned premium valuation parameters from investors from a rigorous commitment to stockholder value (doubling shareholder value every three years) through divestiture of low performing businesses and focus on high potential markets where it can obtain a leading position.

Major recent merger transactions

The acquisition of TBS Group in December 1995 is an example of Lloyds' stockholder value-driven approach to expansion. While TSB was only roughly half the size of Lloyds', extensive care was taken to test customer response to alternative brands and branch structures, create a management team based on meritocracy and build a new retail banking platform. The former head of TSB was named CEO of the combined group to succeed Lloyds' CEO on his retirement. When physical integration was finally permitted by UK legislation in 1999, a combined brand – Lloyds TSB – was chosen for all banking units with the exception of the C & G mortgage brand.

(A) Strategic rationale

The merger permitted Lloyds to expand its extensive branch network in Scotland, a stronghold of TSB, as well as create the opportunity for extensive cost savings from branch overlap and the potential for cross-selling to TSB customers. In addition, the two banks could share the necessary cost of an IT upgrade.

(B) Financial targets

The key financial target established for the merger was cost savings estimated at £400 million annually by 1999, or roughly 11% of the combined group. A commitment was made to achieve these savings with no involuntary redundancies.

In practice, the goal was achieved well within the indicated time frame, while the group has continue to achieve its targeted goals of return over the cost of funds and a declining cost–income ratio. Its 1999 ROE was again over 30%.

MERITANORDBANKEN

Business Profile

The second largest Nordic banking group, MeritaNordbanken combines Nordbanken, Sweden's fourth largest bank with roughly 20% of the retail market, and Merita, Finland's dominant bank with a massive 50% of corporate banking and over 40% of banking assets. Operating with a fully-integrated line of business structure, the group has a strong position in the Nordic fund management market as well as traditional banking in its home markets.

In line with its strategic vision of operating in each of the four Nordic markets, in late 1999 MeritaNordbanken made an agreed take-over bid for Christiania Bank, Norway's second largest. Approval from the Norwegian Ministry of Finance has not yet been obtained.

Major recent merger transactions

The 1997 merger created the first true cross-border fusion of two major European banks and as such is widely seen as the forerunner of similar initiatives. To ensure that the merger is truly one of equals, it has been structured with equal voting rights and earnings attribution enjoyed by stockholders of the two quoted national holding companies, a common management team based in Sweden headed by the former CEO of Nordbanken, and rough balance in the top management team. Major efforts have been made to overcome the substantial cultural barriers between the two firms, although at the retail banking level the two banks still function largely as they did before the merger.

(A) Strategic rationale

The key rationale of the merger was to enable each bank to expand its scope beyond its current market limitations. Nordbanken had had unsuccessful merger talks in Sweden, while Merita's dominance of much smaller Finnish market blunted efforts to expand there. In addition, Merita carried the burden of non-performing loans from an earlier merger as well as a substantial and low yielding real estate portfolio which is now being divested.

The merger also created a market capitalisation which would enable MeritaNordbanken to acquire other Nordic banks to achieve its stated strategic goal of a pan-Nordic entity functioning as a single group.

(B) Financial targets

While cost reduction was a relatively minor dimension of the overall strategic concept, the merger targets cost savings of 4% of combined costs over the three year merger period. Revenue synergies of about 1% of the combined base are also anticipated from cross-selling fund management and insurance products.

SVENSKA HANDELSBANKEN

Business Profile

The largest bank by most measures in the Nordic world, Svenska Handelsbanken is also the only one to have a true Nordic dimension through the opening of retail branches (43 by end 1999) in the other three countries. In its home market of Sweden, the bank has 28% of the lending market and over 30% of the mortgage sector. In Norway and Finland, it is, respectively, the fifth and fourth largest bank in the country. Its superior performance record in most key measures is attributed to a totally decentralised structure in which the local branch is the decision-making centre.

Major recent merger transactions

The February 1997 acquisition of Stadshypotek, the formerly government-controlled mortgage bank, represents the major domestic acquisition made in recent years by Svenska Handelsbanken. Stadshypothek had been losing market share but was acquired in a competitive bid and absorbed into the existing bank structure.

(A) Strategic rationale

Acquisition of Stadshypotek boosted Handelsbanken's market share in the mortgage sector to a dominant 30% following some attrition as a result of the merger. In addition to merger economies, Handelsbanken expects to cross-sell its banking products to virtually all of the over 400,000 Stadshypotek clients who are not customers of the bank.

(B) Financial targets

A remarkable 70% of the acquired company's SK 1 billion in costs will be taken out by the closure of its branch network and other economies. In addition, cross-selling to former Stadshypotek customers will generate substantial but unquantified additional revenues.

UBS AG

Business Profile

UBS (formed from the merger of Swiss Bank Corporation and Union Bank of Switzerland) is Switzerland's largest bank (with market share of 25–35% in key businesses) as well as the world's largest asset manager (with SF 1.6 trillion under management) and a major player in global investment banking. Its private banking unit, which is also the world's largest with over SF 600 billion under management in March 1999, has generated over half of the group's profit in recent years. UBS's domestic banking business generates returns which are relatively low but improving. The Warburg Dillon Read global investment banking unit, which is recovering from losses in 1998, generates over two-thirds of its earnings in Europe.

The group's strategic challenge is to improve profitability (from 10% ROE in 1998 to a targeted 15–20%) through the successful implementation of the 1998 merger.

Major recent merger transactions

The June 1998 fusion of two of Switzerland's three largest banks transformed the competitive positioning of the former SBC, which was the dominant party in the merger. SBC's CEO assumed the same role in the new UBS, which is organised on a line of business basis with most senior positions held by former SBC executives. Following the subsequent 1998 global banking turmoil which severely impacted UBS's investment banking arm, the group's Chairman (formerly CEO of the old UBS) resigned, and major initiatives were taken to transform the risk profile of the group.

(A) Strategic rationale

The merger was designed to improve the competitive positioning of the predecessor banks' major businesses as well as achieve significant operating economies. The new WDR investment banking unit combines two entities which face severe competition from the US-based bulge group firms, while combining the two Swiss branch networks should permit the resulting entity to boost its returns from the historically marginal results.

(B) Financial targets

Cost economies from the merger are projected to exceed those of any other European bank merger: a total of 22% of the pre-merger combined cost base, to be achieved by a 23% reduction in staff globally over a 3–4 year period. Management also set aggregate goals for the merged bank of a 15–20% after tax ROE (against 10% achieved in 1998) and a double-digit average annual earnings per share growth. Most of the staff reductions occurred in the domestic banking network and WDR.

In practice, earnings were severely hit shortly after the merger by market turmoil which generated heavy provisions against risk positions taken by the old UBS and plunged the WDR unit into heavy loss for the year.

UNIBANK

Business Profile

Denmark's second largest banking group, Unibank was formed from a three-way merger in 1990. It has a 27% share of bank lending in the country and a strong presence in the securities sector around its Aros affiliate. While it has not aggressively sought to expand by acquisition in the Nordic region in the banking sector, it acquired the Trevise fund management company in Sweden in 1997 and has a 34% interest in the Polish BWP.

In 1999 Unibank acquired Tryg Baltica, Denmark's largest general insurer and fifth largest life company to create the third largest financial services group in the country.

Major recent merger transactions

The three-way merger creating Unibank in 1990 grouped Privatbanken (a leading corporate and retail bank), SDS (a major savings bank) and the Andelsbanken co-operative group. While Privatbanken supplied the CEO and was the dominant partner in the merger, from the outset each function as well as the 46 retail regions grouped co-heads from each partner bank, and virtually all of the top management teams from these banks were offered posts in the merged group. Implementation was hampered by the four-year period needed to build a new single banking platform as well as asset quality problems stemming from the Nordic recession.

(A) Strategic rationale

The major impulse for the merger was defensive following the announcement of a three-way merger by rival Den Danske Bank. In addition, however, the merger provided the opportunity for cost savings and a platform for expansion both domestically and abroad.

(B) Financial targets

Financial targets for the merger related primarily to cost growth and staff reduction. Expenses would be kept flat for three years, while a 10% staff reduction (by attrition, not forced redundancies) for a three-year period was also targeted, and the branch network was to be cut by 29%. While we understand these targets were achieved, the bank was overtaken by the Nordic banking crisis in 1992, and a new chief executive was brought in to rescue the group.

UNICREDITO ITALIANO

Business Profile

One of the three major banking groups emerging from the rapid consolidation of the Italian banking sector, UniCredito Italiano was formed in 1998 from the merger of the national bank Credito Italiano and Unicredito, a grouping of three former regional savings banks. UniCredito has a 13% share of the total Italian banking market but larger shares in the attractive and wealthy Northern regions of Emilia Romagna, Verona and Piedmont.

The group is being managed on a federal basis with separate local identities, but central IT, product and other functions. It is actively seeking acquisition opportunities both with smaller banks as well as major entities in Italy, and at the same time it is restructuring the existing group to improve productivity and reduce costs. Unicredito is also a leading player in Eastern Europe.

Major recent merger transactions

The October 1998 merger of Credito Italiano with the three former savings banks making up Unicredito brought together a national bank with wholesale capabilities and a group of successful regional banks with solid shares of their local retail markets. Under the leadership of Alessandro Profumo, the merged group has focused on centralising product and IT functions as well as boosting revenues by improving the productivity of the existing staff. The introduction of the former Unicredito stockholders, the three foundations of the former savings banks, has in the past produced some conflict with management over strategy.

(A) Strategic rationale

In a rapidly consolidating environment, the acquisition of Unicredito was a major achievement both to ensure the group with a leading position in the market overall as well as winning significant retail market share in three attractive regions of Northern Italy. At the time of the merger the group was thus the largest Italian bank in terms of market capitalisation, equity and net income as well as the second in assets under management. With its new market cap, UniCredito became well-positioned to bid for other Italian banks as well as knit strategic alliances with other European banks.

(B) Financial targets

The key financial targets set for the merger were aggregate results over the three-year period to the year 2001: improvement in ROE from 7% in 1997 to 20%; reduction in the cost income ratio from 66% to 47% and a tripling of earnings per share. This would be achieved in roughly equal portions by increased revenues and reduced costs. The latter will be slashed by 7% over the period.

WELLS FARGO

Business Profile

The 'new' Wells Fargo with assets in excess of $200 billion was created in 1998 by the merger of two roughly equal size banks, the 'old' Wells and Norwest Corporation. It is a major banking institution in the region West of the Mississippi River with particular strength in California, Texas and Minnesota. It combines Wells' 'high tech' and innovative approach to new distribution channels such as the Internet, supermarket banking and pre-approved loans sold directly to small businesses nationally, with Norwest's 'high touch' emphasis on working closely with consumers and local communities to maximise the value of each relationship as well as leadership in the national mortgage market. Each of the forerunner banks was widely admired as a leader in its particular business model. The merger followed disappointing results when the old Wells merged with First Interstate and lost both considerable customer revenue and market image when attempting substantial cost savings over a limited merger period.

Major recent merger transactions

The formation of the new Wells Fargo in November, 1998 followed an approach to the troubled old Wells by Norwest after the difficult First Interstate merger. An office of the chairman is headed by the former CEO of Norwest, and the business strategy is designed to blend the skills of each predecessor bank with the goal of increasing revenue, particularly in 'Wells West' the former old Wells, by introducing the customer care strategy of 'Wells East', the former Norwest. A relatively long three-year merger period has been chosen to accommodate the necessary IT system development and change the marketing culture of Wells West.

(A) Strategic rationale

In addition to doubling the size of Norwest and giving it access to attractive Western markets such as California and Texas, the merger offered the possibility of applying Norwest's proven cross-selling skills to the customers attracted by the old Wells' innovative distribution strategy.

(B) Financial targets

Given the relative lack of overlap of the two branch networks, the investment needed to build a new retail banking platform and to ensure cultural bonding, the net cost savings are estimated at 8% per annum of the combined cost base after the three-year integration period. While revenue synergies are expected to be significant, no specific estimate was made of such gains.

Notes and References

Chapter 1   The Bank Merger Paradox

1. R. Harold Schroeder (Keefe, Bruyette and Woods), quoted in Smith, 'The Revenue Chase', *Banking Strategies*, Mar/Apr 1998, p. 74.
2. James Hance of Nationsbank quoted in ibid, p. 74.
3. *McKinsey Quarterly*, no. 4, 1997, p. 172.
4. Quoted in Pilloff and Santomero, *Value Effects of Bank Mergers and Acquisitions*, 1996.
5. *Bank for International Settlements Quarterly*.
6. Quoted in Cline, 'Unlocking the Better in Bigger', *Banking Strategies*, Sept/Oct 1998, p. 70.
7. Peristiani, in *Journal of Money, Credit and Banking*, August 1997.
8. Amihud and Miller, *Bank Mergers and Acquisitions*, 1998, p. 60.

Chapter 2   Strategic Positioning

1. Quoted in Cline, 'Unlocking the Better in Bigger', *Banking Strategies*, Sept/Oct 1998, p. 74.

Chapter 3   Cost and Revenue Synergies

1. Smith, 'The Revenue Chase', *Banking Strategies*, Mar/Apr 1999.
2. Blanden, 'Size Does Matter', *The Banker*, June 1998, p. 30.

Chapter 4   Planning the Merger

1. Linder and Crane, 'What It Takes to Make Bank Mergers Pay', *American Banker*, 22 July 1992.
2. Quoted in Dauphinais and Price, *Straight from the CEO*, 1998.
3. Shirreff, 'The Glass Menagerie', *Euromoney*, Sept 1999, p. 216.

Chapter 5   The Due Diligence Process

1. Shirreff, 'Slugfest in Bavaria', *Euromoney*, Dec 1999, p. 92.
2. Cline, 'BankAmerica's Stress Test', *Banking Strategies*, Nov/Dec 1998.

Chapter 6   Leadership

1. See Davis, *Leadership in Financial Institutions*, 1997, for more detailed research.

Chapter 7 Selecting and Motivating People

1. Felman, 'The Accelerated Transition', *Banker's Digest International*, April 1998.
2. Cartwright and Cooper, *Managing Mergers, Acquisitions and Strategic Alliances*, 1992, p. 33.
3. Dauphinais and Price, *Straight from the CEO*, 1998, p. 210.

Chapter 8 Cultural Conflict

1. Salomon Brothers, *European Bank Mergers*, 1992, p. 8.
2. Felman, 'The Accelerated Transition', *Banker's Digest International*, April 1998.
3. Cartwright and Cooper, *Managing Mergers, Acquisitions and Strategic Alliances*, 1992.

Chapter 9 IT Decisions

1. Davis, *Managing Change in the Excellent Banks*, 1989, ch. 4.
2. Cline, 'BankAmerica's Stress Test', *Banking Strategies*, Nov/Dec 1998, p. 26.

Chapter 10 The Bank Merger Score Card

1. Smith Barney, *Mega-Mergers in European Banking*, 1996.

Chapter 11 Case Studies

1. *American Banker*, 20 November 1997.
2. *American Banker*, 27 July 1999.

Chapter 13 Our Own View

1. Haspeslagh, 'Managing the Mating Dance in Equal Mergers', *Financial Times*, 25 October 1999.
2. Davis, *Leadership in Financial Institutions*, 1997.
3. Furash, 'Do It Now?', *Journal of Lending and Credit Risk*, July 1998.
4. Barfield, 'Creating Value through Mergers', *The Banker*, July 1998, p. 24.
5. *Financial Times*, 25 October 1999.
6. Cline, 'Unlocking the Better in Bigger', *Banking Strategies*, Sept/Oct 1998, p. 84.
7. Brown, 'Strategists or Lemmings?', *Banking Strategies*, Sept/Oct 1998.
8. Langohr, 'Big is Not Best in Euroland', *The Banker*, Jan 1998.
9. Furash, 'Do It Now?', *Journal of Lending and Credit Risk*, July 1998.
10. Haspeslagh, 'Managing the Mating Dance in Equal Mergers', *Financial Times*, 25 October 1999.

Bibliography

American Banker, 20 November 1997; 27 July 1999.

Amihud, Yakov and Geoffrey Miller, *Bank Mergers and Acquisitions*, Stern School of Business (Kluwer Academic Publications, Dordrecht, The Netherlands, 1998).

Andersen, Arthur & Co, *The Global Exchange*, April 1998.

Bank for International Settlements Quarterly, August 1999 'Restructuring in the Global Banking Industry' (Basel) pp. 35–48.

Barfield, Richard, 'Creating Value through Mergers', *The Banker*, July 1998 (London) pp. 24–5.

Berger, Allen N. *et al.*, *The Consolidation of the Financial Services Industry: Causes, Consequences and Implications for the Future*, Federal Reserve Board, Number 46, 1998.

Blanden, Michael, 'Size Does Matter', *The Banker*, June 1998 (London) p. 30.

Brown, Thomas, 'Strategists or Lemmings?', *Banking Strategies*, September/October 1998 (Bank Administration Institute, Chicago, IL) pp. 68–82.

Byrd, Edward, 'Pyrrhic Victories?', *Banking Strategies*, March/April 1998 (Bank Administration Institute, Chicago, IL) pp. 74–81.

Calomiris, C. and J. Karenski, *The Bank Merger Wave of the 1990s: Nine Case Studies* (University of Illinois, 1996).

Cartwright, Sue and Cary L. Cooper, *Managing Mergers, Acquisitions and Strategic Alliances*, Manchester School of Management (Reed Educational & Professional Publications Ltd., Oxford, 1992).

Cline, Kenneth, 'Unlocking the Better in Bigger', *Banking Strategies*, September/October 1998 (Bank Administration Institute, Chicago, IL) pp. 84–91.

Cline, Kenneth, 'BankAmerica's Stress Test', *Banking Strategies*, November/December 1998 (Bank Administration Institute, Chicago, IL) pp. 21–4.

Corporate Executive Board, *No End in Sight: Avoiding the 'End Game' Trap in Financial Services* (Washington DC, 1999).

Currie, Antony, 'When Cutting Costs Is Not Enough', *Euromoney*, November 1999 (London) pp. 58–63.

Dauphinais, G. William and Colin Price, *Straight from the CEO: The World's Top Business Leaders Reveal Ideas That Every Manager Can Use* (Simon & Schuster, NY, 1998).

Davis, Steven I., *Managing Change in the Excellent Banks* (Macmillan Press, London, 1989).

Davis, Steven I., *Leadership in Financial Institutions: Lessons for the Future* (Macmillan Press Ltd., London, 1997).

Felman, Mark, 'The Accelerated Transition: Avoiding the Seven Deadly Sins of Post Merger Transition', *Coopers & Lybrand Banker's Digest International (UK)*, April 1998, pp. 15–19.

Financial Times, Inside Track, 25 October 1999, p. 16.

Furash, Edward, 'Do It Now? Guiding Principles for Merger Strategies', *Journal of Lending and Credit Risk*, July 1998 (Philadelphia, PA).

Haspeslagh, Philippe, 'Managing the Mating Dance in Equal Mergers', *Financial Times*, 25 October 1999.

Houston, Joel, 'Value Added by Bank Acquisitions: Lessons from Wells Fargo and First Interstate', *Journal of Applied Corporate Finance*, vol. 9, 1996, pp 74–82.

James, Madeleine *et al.*, 'Playing to the Endgame in Financial Services', *The McKinsey Quarterly*, no. 4, 1997 (McKinsey & Co, NY) pp. 170–85.

Johnson, Hazel, *Bank Mergers, Acquisitions and Strategic Alliances* (Richard D. Irwin, New York, 1995).

Kroll, Karen M., 'Conversion Race', *Banking Strategies*, March/April 1998 (Bank Administration Institute, Chicago, IL) pp. 83–94.

Langohr, Professor Herwig, 'Big is Not Best in Euroland', *The Banker*, January 1998 (London) pp. 27–8.

Linder, Jane and Dwight Crane, 'What It Takes to Make Bank Mergers Pay', *American Banker*, 22 July 1992 (NY).

Peristiani, Stavros, 'Do Mergers Improve the X-Efficiency and Scale Efficiency of U.S. Banks: Evidence from the 1980s', *Journal of Money, Credit and Banking*, vol. 29, no. 3, August 1997 (Ohio State University Press).

Pilloff, Steven J. and Anthony M. Santomero, *The Value Effects of Bank Mergers and Acquisitions* (The Wharton School, October 1996, Philadelphia, PA).

Rhodes, David, 'Do Large Scale Mergers Make Sense?', *Retail Banker International*, 19 August 1997 (London).

Salomon Brothers, *European Bank Mergers: Lessons of Experience for the Future*, May 1992 (London).

Salomon Smith Barney, *European Bank Mergers: Raising the Stakes*, June 1998 (London).

Shirreff, David, 'The Glass Menagerie', *Euromoney*, September 1999 (London) pp. 213–17.

Shirreff, David, 'Slugfest in Bavaria', *Euromoney*, December 1999, pp. 87–92.

Smith Barney, *Mega Mergers in European Banking: A Retrospective and Prospective View*, June 1996 (Smith Barney, NY).

Smith, Kenneth W., 'The Revenue Chase', *Banking Strategies*, March/April 1999 (Chicago, IL) pp. 58–69.

Index

Note: figures and tables are indicated by **emboldened** page numbers.